D1538334

PASS THE
CITIZENSHIP TEST

2020

Angelo Tropea

Reader comments on prior editions

*"My wife teaches a citizenship course and both she and her students love this book!
Good for review by natural citizens, too!"*

"I needed this book to study for my citizenship test. I passed with flying colors. I recommend it to anyone."

"We use this book for our foreign nationals that are becoming US Citizens. They all find it very helpful."

*"One cannot go wrong with this book if you want to pass your citizenship test.
The 100 questions come in various forms. It covers all the history, government and geography questions as well as preparation for the English writing and reading...if one is not fluent in English."*

"This has a good explanation of each question and the book has 3 ways to explain and allow practice of each question. Seems to be better than other choices."

————————————

Copyright 2014-2020 by Angelo Tropea. All rights reserved. No part of this book may be reproduced in any form or by electronic or mechanical means, including information storage and retrieval systems without permission in writing from the publisher.

ISBN: 9781075993008

Credits for illustrations and quoted text are on page 157.

————————

Contents

Naturalization (Citizenship) Interview   1

**To be approved for citizenship, a person must participate
in a citizenship (naturalization) interview with a
USCIS (U.S. Citizenship and Immigration Services) officer.**

What are some things that happen at the naturalization (citizenship) interview?

You can see the official **FREE 16-minute USCIS video** which has an example of the interview by going to the following website:

https://www.uscis.gov/citizenship/learners/study-test

(In the "More Information" box on the right of the page, click on "The USCIS Naturalization Interview and Test Video".)

The video is excellent and has earned high praises from many people.

Among the things you should take to the interview are:

1. N-400 Application (Review it carefully so that you are able to answer questions about it.)
2. Letter with interview appointment notice.

At the interview, the Naturalization (Citizenship) officer will place you under oath. The officer will review with you the N-400 Application for Naturalization) which you filled out and ask questions and review any documents you submitted. The officer will use this review to test your ability to speak and understand the English language.

The officer might ask you questions such as:

- What is your name?
- Have you used any other names?
- Do you legally want to change your name?, etc.

During the interview (either before or after reviewing the N-400 form) the officer will ask civics questions and test your reading and writing ability.

1. The officer may ask up to 10 civics questions. The questions are asked orally and are answered orally. To pass the test, you must answer at least 6 of the questions correctly. (Once you have reached 6 correct answers, the officer will stop asking you civics questions.)

2. For the reading test, the officer will ask you to read up to three simple sentences. You must read at least one sentence correctly to pass.

3. For the writing test, the officer will say up to three sentences. You must write at least one sentence correctly to pass.

At the end of the test, the officer will tell you if you passed, or not.

If you pass, you will be scheduled for the citizenship oath ceremony, which is the final step in the naturalization (citizenship) process.

Three Parts of the Citizenship Test	**2**

Part 1. Civics (History, Government and Geography)

At the citizenship interview you will be asked up to 10 questions from the official 100 questions that the government has provided.

All 100 questions and answers are included in this book - in different ways, to help you remember them!

To pass this part of the test, you must answer correctly at least 6 of the questions. Some of the questions have more than one acceptable answer (For each question, we will suggest what we consider to be the simplest answer - and the easiest to remember.)

Note: Applicants who are 65 or older when they file the Application for Naturalization and who have been legal permanent residents of the United States for 20 or more years, may only need to study 20 questions and answers. We have marked these questions with a star * in this book.

Question numbers:
6, 11, 13, 17, 20, 27, 28, 44, 45, 49
54, 56, 70, 75, 78, 85, 94, 95, 97, 99

The other two parts of the test involve showing some basic ability in English reading and writing. In this book, we will cover all three parts of the exam.

Part 2. English writing

During the citizenship interview, you will be asked to write three (3) sentences containing specific words that the government has announced.

All the <u>writing</u> words (less than 100 words) are listed in this book.

To pass this writing section, you must write one sentence out of the three sentences in a manner that is understandable to the USCIS Officer.

Part 3. English reading

You will be asked to read three (3) sentences containing specific words (less than 100) that the government has announced.

All the <u>reading</u> words (less than 100 words) are also listed in this book.

To pass this reading section, you must read one sentence out of the three sentences in a manner suggesting to the USCIS Officer that you appear to understand the meaning of the sentence.

All 100 USCIS Official Questions in Simple Question-Answer Form	3

1. What is the supreme law of the land?
- *the Constitution*

2. What does the Constitution do?
- *sets up the government*
- *defines the government*
- *protects basic rights of Americans*

3. The idea of self-government is in the first three words of the Constitution. What are these words?
- *We the People*

4. What is an amendment?
- *a change (to the Constitution)*
- *an addition (to the Constitution)*

5. What do we call the first ten amendments to the Constitution?
- *the Bill of Rights*

6. What is one right or freedom from the First Amendment?*
- *Speech*
- *religion*
- *assembly*
- *press*
- *petition the government*

7. How many amendments does the Constitution have?
- *twenty-seven (27)*

8. What did the Declaration of Independence do?
- *announced our independence (from Great Britain)*
- *declared our independence (from Great Britain)*
- *said that the United States is free (from Great Britain)*

9. What are two rights in the Declaration of Independence?
- *Life*
- *liberty*
- *pursuit of happiness*

10. What is freedom of religion?
- *You can practice any religion, or not practice a religion.*

11. What is the economic system in the United States?*
- *capitalist economy*
- *market economy*

12. What is the "rule of law"?
- *Everyone must follow the law.*
- *Leaders must obey the law.*
- *Government must obey the law.*
- *No one is above the law.*

13. Name one branch or part of the government.*
- *Congress (legislative)*
- *President (executive)*
- *the courts (judicial)*

14. What stops one branch of government from becoming too powerful?
- *checks and balances*
- *separation of powers*

15. Who is in charge of the executive branch?
- *the President*

16. Who makes federal laws?

- *Congress*
- *Senate and House (of Representatives)*
- *(U.S. or national) Legislature*

17. What are the two parts of the U.S. Congress?*

- *Senate and House (of Representatives)*

18. How many U.S. Senators are there?

- one hundred (100)

19. We elect a U.S. Senator for how many years?

- *six (6)*

20. Who is one of your state's U.S. Senators now?*

- *Answers depends upon which state you live in. (District of Columbia residents and residents of U.S. territories should answer that D.C. (or the territory where the applicant lives) has no U.S. Senators.)*
  Visit senate.gov to find your state's U.S. Senators.

21. The House of Representatives has how many voting members?

- *four hundred thirty-five (435)*

22. We elect a U.S. Representative for how many years?

- *two (2)*

23. Name your U.S. Representative.

- *Answers depend on where you live. (Residents of territories with Non-voting delegates or resident commissioners may provide the name of that Delegate or Commissioner. Also acceptable is any statement that the territory has no (voting) Representatives in Congress.)*
  Visit house.gov to find your U.S. Representative.

24. Who does a U.S. Senator represent?

- *all people of the state*

25. Why do some states have more Representatives than other states?
- *(because of) the state's population*
- *(because) they have more people*
- *(because) some states have more people*

26. We elect a President for how many years?
- *four (4)*

27. In what month do we vote for President?*
- *November*

28. What is the name of the President of the United States now?*
- *Donald John Trump*
- *Donald Trump*
- *Trump*

29. What is the name of the Vice President of the United States now?
- *Michael Richard Pence*
- *Mike Pence*
- *Pence*

30. If the President can no longer serve, who becomes President?
- *the Vice President*

31. If both the President and the Vice President can no longer serve, who becomes President?
- *the Speaker of the House*

32. Who is the Commander in Chief of the military?
- *the President*

33. Who signs bills to become laws?
- *the President*

34. Who vetoes bills?
- *the President*

35. What does the President's Cabinet do?
- *advises the President*

36. What are two Cabinet-level positions?
- *Secretary of Agriculture*
- *Secretary of Commerce*
- *Secretary of Defense*
- *Secretary of Education*
- *Secretary of Energy*
- *Secretary of Health and Human Services*
- *Secretary of Homeland Security*
- *Secretary of Housing and Urban Development*
- *Secretary of Transportation*
- *Secretary of Veterans Affairs*
- *Secretary of the Treasury*
- *Secretary of the Interior*
- *Secretary of Labor*
- *Secretary of State*
- *Attorney General*
- *Vice President*

37. What does the judicial branch do?
- *reviews laws*
- *explains laws*
- *resolves disputes (disagreements)*
- *decides if a law goes against the Constitution*

38. What is the highest court in the United States?
- *the Supreme Court*

39. How many justices are on the Supreme Court?
- *nine (9)*

40. Who is the Chief Justice of the United States now?
- *John Roberts (John G. Roberts, Jr.)*

41. Under our Constitution, some powers belong to the federal government. What is one power of the federal government?

- *to print money*
- *to declare war*
- *to create an army*
- *to make treaties*

42. Under our Constitution, some powers belong to the states. What is one power of the states?

- *provide schooling and education*
- *provide protection (police, provide safety, fire departments)*
- *give a driver's license*
- *approve zoning and land use*

43. Who is the Governor of your state now?

- *Answers will vary. (District of Columbia residents should answer that D.C. does not have a Governor.)*
  Visit usa.gov/states-and-territories to find the Governor of your state.

44. What is the capital of your state?*

- *Answers vary. (District of Columbia residents should answer that D.C. is not a state and does not have a capital. Residents of U.S. territories should name the capital of the territory.)*

45. What are the two major political parties in the United States?*

- *Democratic and Republican*

46. What is the political party of the President now?

- *Republican (Party)*

47. What is the name of the Speaker of the House of Representatives now?

- *Nancy Pelosi*

48. There are four amendments to the Constitution about who can vote. Describe one of them.
- *Citizens eighteen (18) and older (can vote).*
- *You don't have to pay (a poll tax) to vote.*
- *Any citizen can vote. (Women and men can vote.)*
- *A male citizen of any race (can vote).*

49. What is one responsibility that is only for United States citizens?*
- *serve on a jury*
- *vote in a federal election*

50. Name one right only for United States citizens.
- *vote in a federal election*
- *run for federal office*

51. What are two rights of everyone living in the United States?
- *freedom of expression*
- *freedom of speech*
- *freedom of assembly*
- *freedom to petition the government*
- *freedom of worship*
- *the right to bear arms*

52. What do we show loyalty to when we say the Pledge of Allegiance?
- *the United States*
- *the flag*

53. What is one promise you make when you become a United States citizen?
- *give up loyalty to other countries*
- *defend the Constitution and laws of the United States*
- *obey the laws of the United States*
- *serve in the U.S. military (if needed)*
- *serve (do important work for) the nation (if needed)*
- *be loyal to the United States*

54. How old do citizens have to be to vote for President?*

- *eighteen (18) and older*

55. What are two ways that Americans can participate in their democracy?

- *vote*
- *join a political party*
- *help with a campaign*
- *join a civic group*
- *join a community group*
- *give an elected official your opinion on an issue*
- *call Senators and Representatives*
- *publicly support or oppose an issue or policy*
- *run for office*
- *write to a newspaper*

56. When is the last day you can send in federal income tax forms?*

- *April 15*

57. When must all men register for the Selective Service?

- *at age eighteen (18)*
- *between eighteen (18) and twenty-six (26)*

58. What is one reason colonists came to America?

- *freedom*
- *political liberty*
- *religious freedom*
- *economic opportunity*
- *practice their religion*
- *escape persecution*

59. Who lived in America before the Europeans arrived?

- *American Indians*
- *Native Americans*

60. What group of people was taken to America and sold as slaves?
- *Africans*
- *people from Africa*

61. Why did the colonists fight the British?
- *because of high taxes (taxation without representation)*
- *because the British army stayed in their houses (boarding, quartering)*
- *because they didn't have self-government*

62. Who wrote the Declaration of Independence?
- *(Thomas) Jefferson*

63. When was the Declaration of Independence adopted?
- *July 4, 1776*

64. There were 13 original states. Name three.
- *New Hampshire*
- *Massachusetts*
- *Rhode Island*
- *Connecticut*
- *New York*
- *New Jersey*
- *Pennsylvania*
- *Delaware*
- *Maryland*
- *Virginia*
- *North Carolina*
- *South Carolina*
- *Georgia*

65. What happened at the Constitutional Convention?
- *The Constitution was written.*
- *The Founding Fathers wrote the Constitution.*

66. When was the Constitution written?
- *1787*

67. The Federalist Papers supported the passage of the U.S. Constitution. Name one of the writers.
- *(James) Madison*
- *(Alexander) Hamilton*
- *(John) Jay*
- *Publius*

68. What is one thing Benjamin Franklin is famous for?
- *U.S. diplomat*
- *oldest member of the Constitutional Convention*
- *first Postmaster General of the United States*
- *writer of "Poor Richard's Almanac"*
- *started the first free libraries*

69. Who is the "Father of Our Country"?
- *(George) Washington*

70. Who was the first President?*
- *(George) Washington*

71. What territory did the United States buy from France in 1803?
- *the Louisiana Territory*
- *Louisiana*

72. Name one war fought by the United States in the 1800s.
- *War of 1812*
- *Mexican-American War*
- *Civil War*
- *Spanish-American War*

73. Name the U.S. war between the North and the South.
- *the Civil War*
- *the War between the States*

74. Name one problem that led to the Civil War.
- *slavery*
- *economic reasons*
- *states' rights*

75. What was one important thing that Abraham Lincoln did?*
- *freed the slaves (Emancipation Proclamation)*
- *saved (or preserved) the Union*
- *led the United States during the Civil War*

76. What did the Emancipation Proclamation do?
- *freed the slaves*
- *freed slaves in the Confederacy*
- *freed slaves in the Confederate states*
- *freed slaves in most Southern states*

77. What did Susan B. Anthony do?
- *fought for women's rights*
- *fought for civil rights*

78. Name one war fought by the United States in the 1900s.*
- *World War I*
- *World War II*
- *Korean War*
- *Vietnam War*
- *(Persian) Gulf War*

79. Who was President during World War I?
- *(Woodrow) Wilson*

80. Who was President during the Great Depression and World War II?

- *(Franklin) Roosevelt*

81. Who did the United States fight in World War II?

- *Japan, Germany, and Italy*

82. Before he was President, Eisenhower was a general. What war was he in?

- *World War II*

83. During the Cold War, what was the main concern of the United States?

- *Communism*

84. What movement tried to end racial discrimination?

- *civil rights (movement)*

85. What did Martin Luther King, Jr. do?*

- *fought for civil rights*
- *worked for equality for all Americans*

86. What major event happened on Sept. 11, 2001, in the United States?

- *Terrorists attacked the United States.*

87. Name one American Indian tribe in the United States.

- *Cherokee*
- *Navajo*
- *Sioux*
- *Chippewa*
- *Choctaw*
- *Pueblo*
- *Apache*
- *Iroquois*
- *Creek*
- *Blackfeet*
- *Seminole*
- *Inuit*
- *Cheyenne*
- *Arawak*
- *Shawnee*
- *Mohegan*
- *Huron*
- *Oneida*
- *Lakota*
- *Crow*
- *Teton*
- *Hopi*

88. Name one of the two longest rivers in the United States.

- *Missouri (River)*
- *Mississippi (River)*

89. What ocean is on the West Coast of the United States?

- *Pacific (Ocean)*

90. What ocean is on the East Coast of the United States?

- *Atlantic (Ocean)*

91. Name one U.S. territory.

- *Puerto Rico*
- *U.S. Virgin Islands*
- *American Samoa*
- *Northern Mariana Islands*
- *Guam*

92. Name one state that borders Canada.

- *Maine*
- *New Hampshire*
- *Vermont*
- *New York*
- *Pennsylvania*
- *Ohio*
- *Michigan*
- *Minnesota*
- *North Dakota*
- *Montana*
- *Idaho*
- *Washington*
- *Alaska*

93. Name one state that borders Mexico.

- *California*
- *Arizona*
- *New Mexico*
- *Texas*

94. What is the capital of the United States?*

- *Washington, D.C.*

95. Where is the Statue of Liberty?*
- *New York (Harbor)*
- *Liberty Island*
- *New Jersey*
- *near New York City*
- *on the Hudson (River)*

96. Why does the flag have 13 stripes?
- *because there were 13 original colonies*
- *because the stripes represent the original colonies*

97. Why does the flag have 50 stars?*
- *because there is one star for each state*
- *because each star represents a state*
- *because there are 50 states*

98. What is the name of the national anthem?
- *The Star-Spangled Banner*

99. When do we celebrate Independence Day?*
- *July 4*

100. Name two national U.S. holidays.
- *New Year's Day*
- *Martin Luther King, Jr. Day*
- *Presidents' Day*
- *Memorial Day*
- *Independence Day*
- *Labor Day*
- *Columbus Day*
- *Veterans Day*
- *Thanksgiving*
- *Christmas*

———————————

100 Civics Questions in *Easy-Story* Form

4

This section contains the same 100 questions as in the previous section, but in an *Easy-Story* style which is intended to help you remember.

The **answers** to the questions are displayed in **dark bold letters** to show what you must know to answer the questions asked by the USCIS officer.

Christopher Columbus came to America (the New World) in 1492.

The people who lived in America before Europeans arrived were the American Indians, the native Americans. (Q.59)

They lived in many places and in different groups called tribes.
Some of the Indian tribes were the following: Cherokee, Navajo, Sioux, Chippewa, Choctaw, Pueblo, Apache, Iroquois, Creek, Blackfeet, Seminole, Cheyenne, Arawak, Shawnee, Mohegan, Huron, Oneida, Lakota, Crow, Teton, Hopi, and Inuit. (Q.87)

In Europe in the 1500's and later years there were not many liberties or freedoms or economic opportunities for people to get ahead and live a good life. Because of this, many people (which we call "settlers" or "colonists") came to the New World. Some settled in South America, the Caribbean Islands, and some settled in North America – in what we now call Canada and the United States.

Colonists came to America to get freedom, political liberty, economic opportunity, practice their religion, and escape persecution. (Q.58)

Colonists from Great Britain and other countries settled in the eastern part of what is now the United States. At first, they formed small villages and towns. Slowly, the population grew and spread inland. Great Britain governed this area which we now refer to as the "thirteen colonies."

As a result of the war between the colonists and Great Britain, the thirteen colonies formed into the first 13 American states.

There were thirteen (13) original states: New Hampshire, Massachusetts, Rhode Island, Connecticut, New York, New Jersey, Pennsylvania, Delaware, Maryland, Virginia, North Carolina, South Carolina, and Georgia. (Q.64)

On July 4, 1776, people from 13 British colonies in North America signed a paper called the Declaration of Independence. This paper stated that the 13 colonies were no longer colonies of England and that they were free and independent.

The Declaration of Independence was written by Thomas Jefferson. (Q.62)
Years later, Thomas Jefferson became a President of the United States.
The Declaration of Independence was adopted on July 4, 1776. (Q.63)
The Declaration of Independence: 1) announced our independence (from Great Britain), 2) declared our independence (from Great Britain), 3) said that the United States is free (from Great Britain). (Q.8)
Two rights in the Declaration of Independence are life, liberty, and the pursuit of happiness. (Q.9)

The colonists fought the British because of high taxes (taxation without representation), because the British army stayed in their houses (boarding, quartering), and because they didn't have self-government. (Q.61)

Great Britain (England) did not agree with the colonists trying to be independent from Great Britain. The American Revolutionary war was a result of Britain trying to recapture the colonies.

The Father of Our Country is George Washington. (Q.69) He led the revolutionary army that fought against Great Britain. He also later became the first President of the United States. **The first President was George Washington.** (Q.70)

In 1787 representatives from the 13 colonies wrote the constitution. Soon after that they added 10 changes to the constitution. These changes are called "amendments" to the constitution.

The Constitution was written in 1787. (Q.66)

At the Constitutional Convention, the constitution was written (the founding fathers wrote the constitution). (Q.65)

The federalist papers supported the passage of the Constitution. **The writers of the Federalist Papers were: (James) Madison, (Alexander) Hamilton, (John) Jay, and Publius.** (Q.67)

Because there was disagreement as to what the Constitution should contain, some people proposed that the original Constitution should be changed, or enlarged. They proposed changes which we call "amendments" to the Constitution.

An amendment is a change to the Constitution. (Q.4)

An amendment is an addition to the Constitution. (Q.4)

We call the first ten amendments to the Constitution the "Bill of Rights." (Q. 5)

The constitution and the amendments say many things, including that all people have equal rights and that the government is elected by the people.

The Constitution is the supreme law of the land. (Q.1)

The Constitution sets up the government. (Q.2)

The Constitution defines the government. (Q.2)

The Constitution protects basic rights of Americans. (Q.2)

One freedom guaranteed us by the Constitution is freedom of religion.

Freedom of religion means that you can practice any religion, or not practice a religion. (Q.10)

The idea of self-government is in the first three words of the Constitution.

These three words are "We the People." (Q.3)

The first amendment to the Constitution guarantees certain rights or freedoms. **One right or freedom from the First Amendment is: speech, religion, assembly, press, and petition the government. (Q.6)**

In the United States, we agree that we must live by the rule of law. **The "rule of law" means that: everyone must follow the law, leaders must follow the law, and that no one is above the law. (Q.12)**

As the years passed, more amendments were added to the Constitution. Today the Constitution has twenty-seven (27) amendments. (Q.7)

Under the Constitution some powers belong to the federal government. These powers are to print money, to declare war, to create an army, and to make treaties. (Q.41)

Under the Constitution some powers belong to the states. These powers are to provide schooling and education, provide protection (police), provide safety (fire departments), give a driver's license, and approve zoning and land use. (Q.42)

There are four amendments to the Constitution about who can vote: 1) citizens (18) and older can vote, 2) you don't have to pay a poll tax to vote, 3) any citizen, man or woman, can vote, and 4) a male citizen of any race can vote. (Q.48)

To make sure that no one person or agency has too much power, our government is divided into three (3) parts, or branches.

The branches of our government are: Congress, legislative (President, executive), and the courts (judicial). (Q.13)
The checks and balances, or separation of powers among the three branches stops one branch of government from becoming too powerful. (Q.14)

The President is in charge of the executive branch of government. (Q.15)

The President is elected for four (4) years. (Q.26)

We elect the President in the month of November. (Q.27)

The President is Commander in Chief of the military. (Q.32)

The President signs bills to become laws. (Q.33)

The President can veto bills and stop them from becoming law. (Q.33)

The President appoints people to help him run the government.

The top people become part of his cabinet.

The President's cabinet advises the President. (Q.5)

The following are Cabinet-level positions: Secretary of Agriculture, Secretary of Commerce, Secretary of Defense, Secretary of Education, Secretary of Energy, Secretary of Health and Human Services, Secretary of Homeland Security, Secretary of Housing and Urban Development, Secretary of the Interior, Secretary of Labor, Secretary of State, Secretary of Transportation, Secretary of The Treasury, Secretary of Veterans Affairs, Attorney General, and Vice President. (Q.36)

The name of the President of the United States now is Donald J. Trump. (Q.28)

The name of the Vice President now is Michael Richard Pence. (Q.29)

If the President can no longer serve, the Vice President becomes President. Q.30)

If both the President and the Vice President can no longer serve, the Speaker of the House becomes President. (Q.31)

The judicial branch: reviews laws, explains laws, resolves disputes (disagreements), and decides if a law goes against the Constitution. (Q.37)

The highest court in the United States is the Supreme Court. (Q.38)

There are nine (9) justices on the Supreme Court. (Q.39)

The Chief Justice of the United States is John G. Roberts, Jr. (Q.40)

The two parts of the U.S. Congress are the Senate and the House (of Representatives). (Q.17)

Federal laws are made by Congress (Senate and House of Representatives) also known as the U.S. or national legislature). (Q.16)

There are one hundred (100) U.S. senators. (Q.18)
U.S. Senators represent all the people of their state. (Q.24)
U.S. Senators are elected for six (6) years. (Q.19)

The House of Representatives has 435 voting members. (Q.21)
U.S. Representatives are elected for two (2) years. (Q.22)

Some states have more Representatives than other states because of the state's population, because they have more people, or because some states have more people. (Q.25)

In 1803 the United States bought from France the Louisiana Territory, also known as Louisiana. (Q.71). As the years passed, more states were added to the United States of America. Some states disagreed about such things as slavery.
Africans (people from Africa) were taken to America and sold as slaves. (Q.60)

Problems that led to the Civil War were the following: slavery, economic reasons, and states' rights. (Q.74)

The U.S. war between the North and the South is called the Civil War, or the War between the States. (Q.73) The Civil War lasted from 1861 to 1865. During the civil war, the President was Abraham Lincoln.

The Emancipation Proclamation was issued by President Lincoln. It freed the slaves, freed slaves in Confederate states, freed slaves in the Confederacy, freed slaves in most Southern states. (Q.76)

President Abraham Lincoln: freed the slaves (Emancipation Proclamation), saved (or preserved) the Union, and led the United States during the Civil War. (Q.75)

In the 1800's the United States fought several wars: The War of 1812, the Mexican-American War, the Civil War, and the Spanish-American War. (Q.72)

In the 1900's the United States fought several wars: World War I, World War II, Korean War, Vietnam War, and the (Persian) Gulf War. (Q.78)

During the First World War, the President was (Woodrow) Wilson. (Q.79)

During the Great Depression and World War II, the President was (Franklin) Roosevelt. (Q.80)

During World War II, the United States fought Japan, Italy, and Germany. (Q.81). During World War II, Eisenhower was a general. (Q.82)

During the Cold War, the main concern of the United States was Communism. (Q.83)

The civil rights movement tried to end discrimination. (Q.84)

During our history, there were many leaders trying to improve our country. Martin Luther King fought for civil rights, worked for equality of all Americans. (Q.85)

On September 11, 2001, terrorists attacked the United States. (Q.86)

_____

Benjamin Franklin is famous for being a U.S. diplomat, the oldest member of the Constitutional Convention, first Postmaster General of the United States, writer of "Poor Richard's Almanac, and for starting the first free libraries. (Q.68)

Susan B. Anthony fought for women's rights, fought for civil rights. (Q.77)

_____

The two major political parties in the United States are the Republican party and the Democratic party. (Q.45)

The political party of the President now (Donald J. Trump) is the Republican party. (Q.46)

The name of the Speaker of the House of Representatives is Nancy Pelosi. (Q.47)

A responsibility of an American citizen is 1) to vote in a federal election, and 2) serve on a jury. (Q.49)

A right of an American Citizen is 1) to vote in a federal election, and 2) run for federal office. (Q.50)

A citizen has to be eighteen (18) or older to vote for President. (Q.54)

Two rights of everyone living in the United States are: freedom of expression, freedom of speech, freedom of assembly, freedom to petition the government, freedom of worship, and the right to bear arms. (Q.51)

One promise you make when you become a United States citizen is
1) give up loyalty to other countries
2) defend the Constitution and laws of the United States
3) obey the laws of the United States
4) serve in the U.S. military (if needed)
5) serve (do important work for) the nation (if needed), and
6) be loyal to the United States. (Q.53)

We show loyalty to the flag when we say the Pledge of Allegiance. (Q.52)

Two ways that Americans can participate in their democracy are:
1) vote
2) join a political party
3) help with a campaign
4) join a civic group
5) join a community group
6) give an elected official your opinion on an issue
7) call Senators and Representatives
8) publicly support or oppose an issue or policy
9) run for office, and
10) write to a newspaper (Q.55)

The last day to send in a federal tax return is April 15. (Q.56)

All men must register for the selective service at age eighteen (18). (Q.48)

In the United States, we believe in freedom to conduct business.

The economic system in the United States is: a capitalist economy, a market economy. (Q.11)

———

The following four questions relate to your specific state. All the answers that are specific to your state are listed in this book.

(Q.20) Who is one of your state's U.S. Senators now?

Answers will vary. (District of Columbia residents and residents of U.S. territories should answer that D.C. (or territory where applicant lives) has no U.S, Senators. (See page 152 for list of Senators.)

(Q.23) Name your U.S. Representative.

(Residents of territories with nonvoting Delegates or Resident Commissioners may provide the name of the Delegate or Commissioner. Also acceptable is any statement that the territory has no (voting) Representatives in Congress.) (See page 148 for U.S. Representatives.)

(Q.43) Who is the Governor of your state now?

(District of Columbia residents should answer that D.C. does not have a Governor.) (See page 155 for list of Governors.)

(Q.44) What is the capital of your state?

(District of Columbia residents should answer that D.C. is not a state and does not have a capital. Residents of U.S. territories should name the Capital of the territory.) (See page 154 for list of state capitals.)

Questions 88 – 100 relate to geography, American symbols, and Holidays.

88. Name one of the two longest rivers in the United States.

Missouri (River)

Mississippi (River)

89. What ocean is on the West Coast of the United States?

Pacific (Ocean)

90. What ocean is on the East Coast of the United States?

Atlantic (Ocean)

91. Name one U.S. territory.

Puerto Rico, U.S. Virgin Islands, American Samoa, Northern Mariana, Islands, Guam

92. Name one state that borders Canada.

Maine	Michigan
New Hampshire	Minnesota
Vermont	Montana
New York	Idaho
Pennsylvania	Washington
Ohio,	Alaska
North Dakota	

93. Name one state that borders Mexico.

California, Arizona, New Mexico, Texas

94. What is the capital of the United States?

Washington, D.C.

95. Where is the Statue of Liberty?

New York (Harbor), Liberty Island, New Jersey, near New York City, and on the Hudson (River).

96. Why does the flag have 13 stripes?

because there were 13 original colonies,

because the stripes represent the original colonies

97. Why does the flag have 50 stars?

because there is one star for each state, because each star represents a

state, because there are 50 states

98. What is the name of the national anthem?

The Star-Spangled Banner

99. When do we celebrate Independence Day?

July 4

100. Name two national U.S. holidays.

New Year's Day	Columbus Day
Martin Luther King, Jr. Day	Veterans Day
Presidents' Day, Memorial Day	Thanksgiving
Independence Day	Christmas
Labor Day	

_____

100 Questions, USCIS Official Lessons(9) and Suggestions on Remembering

5

Explanation

The following pages contain the **USCIS 100 official questions and answers.**

The question is on the card on the left and the answer is on the card on the right.

Beneath the cards is the **Official USCIS Civics Lesson**(9). The USCIS provides these lessons to help you remember the answers.

After most official civics lessons, there is a shorter *Easy* **Lesson** that is meant to provide in simpler form some of the more important facts in the official lesson.

The *Easy Answer!* is an example of one of the **easy** ways to answer and remember the question.

We suggest that you read the question out loud and then try to answer it out loud. This way you will get used to the sound of the question and the sound of the answer. This will help you remember the question and answer.

If English is not your native language, have a friend or relative who speaks English study with you. Let your friend or relative read the question, and then try to answer it. Ask your friend or relative if you are pronouncing the answer correctly. Say the *Easy Answer* over and over until you are comfortable with it and have it completely memorized.

Try to review the questions and answers every day. You will be surprised at how easy it will be to remember all the questions and answers!

Q. 1	A. 1
What is the supreme law of the land?	• *the Constitution*

Official USCIS Civics lesson

The Founding Fathers of the United States wrote the Constitution in 1787. The constitution is the "supreme law of the land." The U.S. Constitution has lasted longer than any other country's constitution. It establishes the basic principles of the United States government. The Constitution establishes a system of government called "representative democracy." In a representative democracy, citizens choose representatives to make the laws. U.S. citizens also choose a president to lead the executive branch of government. The Constitution lists fundamental rights for all citizens and other people living in the United States. Laws made in the United States must follow the Constitution.

Easy **Lesson**

The Constitution is the supreme law of the U. S. It was written in 1787 by the leaders of our government. It lists the rights of people who live in the U. S. It says that all laws in the U. S. must follow the Constitution. You can see the original Constitution at the National Archives museum in Washington, D.C.

Easy Answer!

The supreme law of the land is the Constitution.

U.S. Constitution (1)

Q. 2	A. 2
What does the Constitution do?	• *sets up the government* • *defines the government* • *protects basic rights of Americans*

Official USCIS Civics lesson

The Constitution of the United States divides government power between the national government and state governments. The name for this division of power is "federalism." Federalism is an important idea in the Constitution. We call the Founding Fathers who wrote the Constitution the "Framers" of the Constitution. The Framers wanted to limit the powers of the government, so they separated the powers into three branches: executive, legislative, and judicial. The Constitution explains the power of each branch. The Constitution also includes changes and additions, called "amendments." The first 10 amendments are called the "Bill of Rights." The Bill of Rights established the individual rights and liberties of all Americans.

Easy Lesson

The Constitution divides government power into two parts: national government and state governments. It also limits the power of each part by dividing the powers into three parts called "branches" (executive, legislative and judicial). The Constitution is made up of the original Constitution plus changes and additions called "amendments." The first 10 amendments, called the "Bill of Rights," established the rights and liberties of all Americans.

Easy Answer!

The Constitution sets up the government.

Q. 3	A. 3
The idea of self-government is in the first three words of the Constitution. What are these words?	• **_We the People_**

Official USCIS Civics lesson

The Constitution says: "We the People of the United States, in Order to form a more perfect Union, establish Justice, insure domestic Tranquility, provide for the common defense, promote the general Welfare, and secure the Blessings of Liberty to ourselves and our Posterity, do ordain and establish this Constitution for the United States of America." With the words "We the People," the Constitution states that the people set up the government. The government works for the people and protects the rights of people. In the United States, the power to govern comes from the people, who are the highest power. This is called "popular sovereignty." The people elect representatives to make laws.

Easy Lesson

The first three words of the Constitution "We the people" make clear that the people set up the government. The power of government comes from the people, who are the highest power. The people elect representatives to make laws. The government works for the people and protects the rights of people.

Easy Answer!

The first three words of the Constitution are "We the People".

Q. 4	A. 4
What is an amendment?	• *a change (to the Constitution)* • *an addition (to the Constitution)*

Official USCIS Civics lesson

An amendment is a change or addition to the Constitution. The Framers of the Constitution knew that laws can change as a country grows. They did not want to make it too easy to modify the Constitution, the supreme law of the land. The Framers also did not want the Constitution to lose its meaning. For this reason, the Framers decided that Congress could pass amendments in only two ways: by a two-thirds vote in the U.S. Senate and the House of Representatives or by a special convention. A special convention has to be requested by two-thirds of the states. After an amendment has passed in Congress or by a special convention, the amendment must then be ratified (accepted) by the legislatures of three-fourths of the states. The amendment can also be ratified by a special convention in three-fourths of the states. Not all proposed amendments are ratified. Six times in U.S. history amendments have passed in Congress but were not approved by enough states to be ratified.

***Easy* Lesson**

An amendment is a change or addition to the Constitution. The Constitution specifies how an amendment can be made and added to the Constitution.

Easy Answer!

An amendment is a change to the Constitution.

Q. 5	A. 5
What do we call the first ten amendments to the Constitution?	• *the Bill of Rights*

Official USCIS Civics lesson

The Bill of Rights is the first 10 amendments to the Constitution. When the Framers wrote the Constitution, they did not focus on individual rights. They focused on creating the system and structure of government. Many Americans believed that the Constitution should guarantee the rights of the people, and they wanted a list of all the things a government could not do. They were afraid that a strong government would take away the rights people won in the Revolutionary War. James Madison, one of the Framers of the Constitution, wrote a list of individual rights and limits on the government. These rights appear in the first 10 amendments, called the Bill of Rights. Some of these rights include freedom of expression, the right to bear arms, freedom from search without warrant, freedom not to be tried twice for the same crime, the right to not testify against yourself, the right to a trial by a jury of your peers, the right to an attorney, and protection against excessive fines and unusual punishments. The Bill of Rights was ratified in 1791.

Easy Lesson

The Bill of Rights is the first 10 amendments to the Constitution. The amendments protect individual rights and place limits on the power of government.

Easy Answer!

The first ten amendments are called the "Bill of Rights".

Q. 6	A. 6
What is <u>one</u> right or freedom from the First Amendment?*	• *speech* • *religion* • *assembly* • *press* • *petition the government*

Official USCIS Civics lesson

The First Amendment of the Bill of Rights protects a person's right to freedom of expression. Freedom of expression allows open discussion and debate on public issues. Open discussion and debate are important to democracy. The First Amendment also protects freedom of religion and free speech. This amendment says that Congress may not pass laws that establish an official religion and may not limit religious expression. Congress may not pass laws that limit freedom of the press or the right of people to meet peacefully. The First Amendment also gives people the right to petition the government to change laws or acts that are not fair. Congress may not take away these rights. The First Amendment of the Constitution guarantees and protects these rights.

Easy **Lesson**

The First Amendment of the Constitution guarantees and protects freedom of speech and other rights.

Easy Answer!

One freedom guaranteed by the First Amendment is freedom of speech.

Q. 7	A. 7
How many amendments does the Constitution have?	• *twenty-seven (27)*

Official USCIS Civics lesson

The first 10 amendments to the Constitution are called the Bill of Rights. They were added in 1791. Since then, 17 more amendments have been added. The Constitution currently has 27 amendments. The 27th Amendment was added in 1992. It explains how senators and representatives are paid. Interestingly, Congress first discussed this amendment back in 1789 as one of the original amendments considered for the Bill of Rights.

Easy **Lesson**

There are 27 amendments to the Constitution. These amendments include the first 10 amendments which are known as the "Bill Of Rights".

Easy Answer!

The Constitution has 27 amendments.

Q. 8	A. 8
What did the Declaration of Independence do?	• *announced our independence (from Great Britain)* • *declared our independence (from Great Britain)* • *said that the United States is free (from Great Britain)*

Official USCIS Civics lesson

The Declaration of Independence contains important ideas about the American system of government. The Declaration of Independence states that all people are created equal and have "certain unalienable rights." These are rights that no government can change or take away. The author of the Declaration, Thomas Jefferson, wrote that the American colonies should be independent because Great Britain did not respect the basic rights of people in the colonies. Jefferson believed that a government exists only if the people think it should. He believed in the idea that the people create their own government and consent, or agree, to follow laws their government makes. This idea is called "consent of the governed." If the government creates laws that are fair and protect people, then people will agree to follow those laws. In the Declaration of Independence, Jefferson wrote a list of complaints the colonists had against the King of England. Jefferson ended the Declaration with the statement that the colonies are, and should be, free and independent states. The Second Continental Congress voted to accept the Declaration on July 4, 1776.

***Easy* Lesson**

The Declaration of Independence was written by Thomas Jefferson and accepted by the Second Continental Congress on July 4, 1776. It announced our independence from Great Britain (England) and also contains important ideas about the American system of government.

Easy Answer!

The Declaration of Independence announced our independence from Great Britain.

Q. 9	A. 9
What are <u>two</u> rights in the Declaration of Independence?	• **Life** • **liberty** • **pursuit of happiness**

Official USCIS Civics lesson

The Declaration of Independence lists three rights that the Founding Fathers considered to be natural and "unalienable." They are the right to life, liberty, and the pursuit of happiness. These ideas about freedom and individual rights were the basis for declaring America's independence. Thomas Jefferson and the other Founding Fathers believed that people are born with natural rights that no government can take away. Government exists to protect these rights. Because the people voluntarily give up power to a government, they can take that power back. The British government was not protecting the rights of the colonists, so the colonies took back their power and separated from Great Britain.

Easy **Lesson**

The Declaration of Independence lists three rights that the Founding Fathers considered to be natural and "unalienable" (cannot be taken away). They are the right to life, liberty, and the pursuit of happiness.

Easy Answer!

Two rights in the Declaration of Independence are life and liberty.

Declaration of Independence (2)

Q. 10	A. 10
What is freedom of religion?	• *You can practice any religion, or not practice a religion.*

Official USCIS Civics lesson

Colonists from Spain, France, Holland, England, and other countries came to America for many different reasons. One of the reasons was religious freedom. The rulers of many of these countries told their citizens that they must go to a certain church and worship in a certain way. Some people had different religious beliefs than their rulers and wanted to have their own churches. In 1620, the Pilgrims were the first group that came to America seeking religious freedom. Religious freedom was also important to the Framers. For this reason, freedom of religion was included in the Constitution as part of the Bill of Rights. The First Amendment to the Constitution guarantees freedom of religion. The First Amendment states, "Congress shall make no law respecting an establishment of religion, or prohibiting the free exercise thereof." The First Amendment also prohibits Congress from setting up an official U.S. religion, and protects citizens' rights to hold any religious belief, or none at all.

Easy Lesson

One reason why colonists came to America was religious freedom. The First Amendment prohibits Congress from setting up an official U.S. religion, and protects the rights of citizens to hold any religious belief, or none at all.

Easy Answer!

Religious freedom means the right to practice any religion, or not practice a religion.

Q. 11	A. 11
What is the economic system in the United States?*	• *capitalist economy* • *market economy*

Official USCIS Civics lesson

___

The economic system of the United States is capitalism. In the American economy, most businesses are privately owned. Competition and profit motivate businesses. Businesses and consumers interact in the called a "market economy." In a market economy, businesses decide what to produce, how much to produce, and what to charge. Consumers decide what, when, and where they will buy goods or services. In a market economy, competition, supply, and demand influence the decisions of businesses and consumers.

Easy Lesson

___

In the American economy, most businesses are privately owned. Competition, supply, and demand influence the decisions of businesses and consumers.

Easy Answer!

___

The economic system in the United States is a capitalist economy.

Q. 12	A. 12
What is the "rule of law"?	• **Everyone must follow the law.** • **Leaders must obey the law.** • **Government must obey the law.** • **No one is above the law.**

Official USCIS Civics lesson

John Adams was one of the Founding Fathers and the second president of the United States. He wrote that our country is, "a government of laws, and not of men." No person or group is above the law. The rule of law means that everyone (citizens and leaders) must obey the laws. In the United States, the U.S. Constitution is the foundation for the rule of law. The United States is a "constitutional democracy" (a democracy with a constitution). In constitutional democracies, people are willing to obey the laws because the laws are made by the people through their elected representatives. If all people are governed by the same laws, the individual rights and liberties of each person are better protected. The rule of law helps to make sure that government protects all people equally and does not violate the rights of certain people.

Easy **Lesson**

The rule of law means that everyone (citizens and leaders) must obey the laws. The rule of law helps to make sure that government protects all people equally and does not violate the rights of people.

Easy Answer!

The rule of law means that no one is above the law.

Q. 13	A. 13
Name <u>one</u> branch or part of the government.*	• **Congress** • **legislative** • **President** • **executive** • **the courts** • **judicial**

Official USCIS Civics lesson

The Constitution establishes three branches of government: legislative, executive, and judicial. Article I of the Constitution establishes the legislative branch. Article I explains that Congress makes laws. Congress (the Senate and the House of Representatives) is the legislative branch of the U.S. government. Article II of the Constitution establishes the executive branch. The executive branch enforces the laws that Congress passes. The executive branch makes sure all the people follow the laws of the United States. The president is the head of the executive branch. The vice president and members of the president's cabinet are also part of the executive branch. Article III of the Constitution establishes the judicial branch. The judicial branch places the highest judicial power in the Supreme Court. One responsibility of the judicial branch is to decide if government laws and actions follow the Constitution. This is a very important responsibility.

Easy **Lesson**

The three branches of government are: legislative, executive, and judicial. The legislative branch (Congress) makes laws. The executive branch (President) enforces the laws that Congress passes. The judicial branch places the highest judicial power in the Supreme Court. The judicial branch decides if government laws and actions follow the Constitution.

Easy Answer!

One branch of the government is the President.

Q. 14	A. 14
What stops one branch of government from becoming too powerful?	• *checks and balances* • *separation of powers*

Official USCIS Civics lesson

The Constitution separates the government's power into three branches to prevent one person or group from having too much power. The separation of government into three branches creates a system of checks and balances. This means that each branch can block, or threaten to block, the actions of the other branches. Here are some examples: the Senate (part of the legislative branch) can block a treaty signed by the president (the executive branch). In this example, the legislative branch is "checking" the executive. The U.S. Supreme Court (the judicial branch) can reject a law passed by Congress (the legislative branch). In this example, the judicial branch is "checking" the legislative branch. This separation of powers limits the power of the government and prevents the government from violating the rights of the people.

Easy **Lesson**

The separation of government into three branches creates a system of checks and balances. This separation of powers limits the power of the government and prevents the government from violating the rights of the people

Easy Answer!

The separation of powers stops one part of government from becoming too powerful.

Q. 15	A. 15
Who is in charge of the executive branch?	• *the President*

Official USCIS Civics lesson

The job of the executive branch is to carry out, or execute, federal laws and enforce laws passed by Congress. The head of the executive branch is the president. The president is both the head of state and the head of government. The president's powers include the ability to sign treaties with other countries and to select ambassadors to represent the United States around the world. The president also sets national policies and proposes laws to Congress. The president names the top leaders of the federal departments. When there is a vacancy on the Supreme Court, the president names a new member. However, the Senate has the power to reject the president's choices. This limit on the power of the president is an example of checks and balances.

***Easy* Lesson**

The head of the executive branch is the president. The president signs treaties, selects ambassadors, sets national policies and proposes laws to Congress. The president names the top leaders of the federal departments and nominates a person when there is a vacancy on the Supreme Court.

Easy Answer!

The President is in charge of the Executive Branch.

Q. 16	A. 16
Who makes federal laws?	• **Congress** • **Senate and House (of Representatives)** • **(U.S. or national) Legislature**

Official USCIS Civics lesson

Congress makes federal laws. A federal law usually applies to all states and all people in the United States. Either side of Congress—the Senate or the House of Representatives—can propose a bill to address an issue. When the Senate proposes a bill, it sends the bill to a Senate committee. The Senate committee studies the issue and the bill. When the House of Representatives proposes a bill, it sends the bill to a House of Representatives committee. The committee studies the bill and sometimes makes changes to it. Then the bill goes to the full House or Senate for consideration. When each chamber passes its own version of the bill, it often goes to a "conference committee." The conference committee has members from both the House and the Senate. This committee discusses the bill, tries to resolve the differences, and writes a report with the final version of the bill. Then the committee sends the final version of the bill back to both houses for approval. If both houses approve the bill, it is considered "enrolled." An enrolled bill goes to the president to be signed into law. If the president signs the bill, it becomes a federal law.

Easy Lesson

Either side of Congress—the Senate or the House of Representatives—can propose a bill to address an issue. If both houses approve the bill, it goes to the president to be signed into law. If the president signs the bill, it becomes a federal law.

Easy Answer!

Congress makes federal laws.

Q. 17	A. 17
What are the two parts of the U.S. Congress?*	• **Senate, and** **House (of Representatives)**

Official USCIS Civics lesson

Congress is divided into two parts - the Senate and the House of Representatives. Because it has two "chambers," the U.S. Congress is known as a "bicameral" legislature. The system of checks and balances works in Congress. Specific powers are assigned to each of these chambers. For example, only the Senate has the power to reject a treaty signed by the president or a person the president chooses to serve on the Supreme Court. Only the House of Representatives has the power to introduce a bill that requires Americans to pay taxes.

***Easy* Lesson**

Congress is divided into two parts - the Senate and the House of Representatives. The system of checks and balances works in Congress and limits the power of each part.

Easy Answer!

The two parts of Congress are the Senate and the House of Representatives.

Capitol Building (3)

A. 18

*How many U.S. Senators
are there?*

A. 18

• *one hundred (100)*

Official USCIS Civics lesson

There are 100 senators in Congress, two from each state. All states have equal power in the Senate because each state has the same number of senators. States with a very small population have the same number of senators as states with very large populations. The Framers of the Constitution made sure that the Senate would be small. This would keep it more orderly than the larger House of Representatives. As James Madison wrote in Federalist Paper #63, the Senate should be a "temperate and respectable body of citizens" that operates in a "cool and deliberate" way.

***Easy* Lesson**

There are 100 senators in Congress, two from each state.

Easy Answer!

There are 100 U.S. Senators.

Senate (4)

Q. 19	A. 19
We elect a U.S. Senator for how many years?	• *six (6)*

Official USCIS Civics lesson

The Framers of the Constitution wanted senators to be independent from public opinion. They thought a fairly long, six-year term would give them this protection. They also wanted longer Senate terms to balance the shorter two-year terms of the members of the House, who would more closely follow public opinion. The Constitution puts no limit on the number of terms a senator may serve. Elections for U.S. senators take place on even-numbered years. Every two years, one-third of the senators are up for election.

Easy **Lesson**

Senators serve for six years. Because of this, they are more independent of public opinion than Representatives who serve for two years.

Easy Answer!

We elect U.S. Senators for six (6) years.

Q. 20	A. 20
Who is <u>one</u> of your state's U.S. Senators now?*	*Answers depends upon which state you live in. (District of Columbia residents and residents of U.S. territories should answer that D.C. (or the territory where the applicant lives) has no U.S. Senators.) Visit senate.gov to find your state's U.S. Senators.*

Official USCIS Civics lesson

_____

For a complete list of U.S. senators and the states they represent, go to www.senate.gov.

Easy Answer!

_____

One of my state's U.S. Senator is _____.

(See list of U.S. Senators on page 152.)

Q. 21	A. 21
The House of Representatives has how many voting members?	• *four hundred thirty-five (435)*

Official USCIS Civics lesson

The House of Representatives is the larger chamber of Congress. Since 1912, the House of Representatives has had 435 voting members. However, the distribution of members among the states has changed over the years. Each state must have at least one representative in the House. Beyond that, the number of representatives from each state depends on the population of the state. The Constitution says that the government will conduct a census of the population every 10 years to count the number of people in each state. The results of the census are used to recalculate the number of representatives each state should have. For example, if one state gains many residents that state could get one or more new representatives. If another state loses residents, that state could lose one or more. But the total number of voting U.S. representatives does not change.

***Easy* Lesson**

Each state must have at least one representative in the House. Beyond that, the number of representatives from each state depends on the population of the state. The total number of Representatives is 435.

Easy Answer!

The House of Representatives has 435 voting members.

Q. 22	A. 22
We elect a U.S. Representative for how many years?	• *two (2)*

Official USCIS Civics lesson

People who live in a representative's district are called "constituents." Representatives tend to reflect the views of their constituents. If representatives do not do this, they may be voted out of office. The Framers of the Constitution believed that short two-year terms and frequent elections would keep representatives close to their constituents, public opinion, and more aware of local and community concerns. The Constitution puts no limit on the number of terms a representative may serve. All representatives are up for election every two years.

***Easy* Lesson**

U.S. Representatives serve for short 2-year terms before they have to run for reelection. This encourages them to constantly stay in touch and reflect the views of the people that voted them in.

Easy Answer!

We elect U.S. Representatives for two (2) years.

Q. 23	A. 23
Name your U.S. Representative.	*Answers depends on where you live. (Residents of territories with Non-voting delegates or resident commissioners may provide name of that Delegate or Commissioner. Also acceptable is any statement that the territory has no (voting) Representatives in Congress.) Visit house.gov to find your U.S. Representative.*

Official USCIS Civics lesson

For a complete list of U.S. representatives and the districts they represent, go to www.house.gov.

Easy Answer!

The name of my U.S. Representative is _____.

(See list of U.S. Representatives on page 148.)

Q. 24	A. 24
Who does a U.S. Senator represent?	• *all people of the state*

Official USCIS Civics lesson

Senators are elected to serve the people of their state for six years. Each of the two senators represents the entire state. Before the 17th Amendment to the Constitution was ratified in 1913, the state legislatures elected the U.S. senators to represent their state. Now, all the voters in a state elect their two U.S. senators directly.

***Easy* Lesson**

There are 2 U.S. Senators for each state. They are elected by all the voters in their state.

Easy Answer!

A U.S. Senator represents all the voters of the state.

Q. 25	A. 25
Why do some states have more Representatives than other states?	• *(because of) the state's population* • *(because) they have more people* • *(because) some states have more people*

Official USCIS Civics lesson

The Founding Fathers wanted people in all states to be represented fairly. In the House of Representatives, a state's population determines the number of representatives it has. In this way, states with many people have a stronger voice in the House. In the Senate, every state has the same number of senators. This means that states with few people still have a strong voice in the national government.

Easy **Lesson**

A state's population determines the number of representatives it has.

Easy Answer!

Some states have more Representatives than other states because some states have more people.

Q. 26	A. 26
We elect a President for how many years?	• *four (4)*

Official USCIS Civics lesson

Early American leaders thought that the head of the British government, the king, had too much power. Because of this, they limited the powers of the head of the new U.S. government. They decided that the people would elect the president every four years. The president is the only official elected by the entire country through the Electoral College. The Electoral College is a process that was designed by the writers of the Constitution to select presidents. It came from a compromise between the president being elected directly by the people and the president being chosen by Congress. Citizens vote for electors, who then choose the president. Before 1951, there was no limit on the number of terms a president could serve. With the 22nd Amendment to the Constitution, the president can only be elected to two terms (four years each) for a total of eight years.

Easy Lesson

Early American leaders decided that the people would elect the president every four years. The president is the only official elected by the entire country through the Electoral College. The president can only be elected to two terms (four years each) for a total of eight years.

Easy Answer!

We elect a President for four years.

Q. 27	A. 27
In what month do we vote for President?*	• *November*

Official USCIS Civics lesson

The Constitution did not set a national election day. In the past, elections for federal office took place on different days in different states. In 1845, Congress passed legislation to designate a single day for all Americans to vote. It made Election Day the Tuesday after the first Monday in November. Congress chose November because the United States was mostly rural. By November, farmers had completed their harvests and were available to vote. Another reason for this date was the weather. People were able to travel because it was not yet winter. They chose Tuesday for Election Day so that voters had a full day after Sunday to travel to the polls.

Easy Lesson

Election Day is the Tuesday after the first Monday in November.

Easy Answer!

We vote for President in the month of November.

Q. 28	A. 28
What is the name of the President of the United States now?*	• *Donald J. Trump* • *Donald Trump* • *Trump*

Official USCIS Civics lesson

Visit uscis.gov/citizenship/testupdates for the name of the President of the United States.

For more information about the president of the United States, visit whitehouse.gov.

Easy Answer!

The name of the President now is Donald Trump.

Q. 29	A. 29
What is the name of the Vice President of the United States now?	• *Michael R. Pence* • *Mike Pence* • *Pence*

Official USCIS Civics lesson

Visit uscis.gov/citizenship/testupdates for the name of the Vice President of the United States. For more information about the vice president of the United States, visit whitehouse.gov.

Easy Answer!

The name of the Vice President now is Mike Pence.

Q. 30	A. 30
If the President can no longer serve, who becomes President?	• *the Vice President*

Official USCIS Civics lesson

If the president dies, resigns, or cannot work while still in office, the vice president becomes president. For this reason, the qualifications for vice president and president are the same. A vice president became president nine times in U.S. history when the president died or left office. William Henry Harrison died in office in 1841. Zachary Taylor died in office in 1850. Abraham Lincoln was killed in office in 1865. James Garfield was killed in office in 1881. William McKinley was killed in office in 1901. Warren Harding died in office in 1923. Franklin Roosevelt died in office in 1945. John F. Kennedy was killed in office in 1963. Richard Nixon resigned from office in 1974. No one other than the vice president has ever succeeded to the presidency.

Easy Lesson

If the president dies, resigns, or cannot work while still in office, the vice president becomes president.

Easy Answer!

If the President can no longer serve, the Vice President becomes President.

Q. 31	A. 31
If both the President and the Vice President can no longer serve, who becomes President?	• *the Speaker of the House*

Official USCIS Civics lesson

If both the president and vice president cannot serve, the next person in line is the speaker of the House of Representatives. This has not always been the procedure. Soon after the country was founded, a law was passed that made the Senate president pro tempore the next in line after the president and vice president. The president pro tempore presides over the Senate when the vice president is not there. Later in U.S. history, the secretary of state was third in line. With the Presidential Succession Act of 1947, Congress returned to the original idea of having a congressional leader next in line. In 1967, the 25th Amendment was ratified. It established procedures for presidential and vice presidential succession.

Easy **Lesson**

If both the president and vice president cannot serve, the next person in line is the Speaker of the House of Representatives. The 25th Amendment established procedures for presidential and vice presidential succession.

Easy Answer!

If both the President and the Vice President can no longer serve, the Speaker of the House becomes President.

Q. 32	A. 32
Who is the Commander in Chief of the military?	● **the President**

Official USCIS Civics lesson

The Founding Fathers strongly believed in republican ideals. A republic is a government where a country's political power comes from the citizens, not the rulers, and is put into use by representatives elected by the citizens. That is why they made the president the commander in chief. They wanted a civilian selected by the people. They did not want a professional military leader. The president commands the armed forces, but Congress has the power to pay for the armed forces and declare war. In 1973, many members of Congress believed that the president was misusing or abusing his powers as commander in chief. They thought that the president was ignoring the legislative branch and not allowing the system of checks and balances to work. In response, Congress passed the War Powers Act. The War Powers Act gave Congress a stronger voice in decisions about the use of U.S. troops. President Richard Nixon vetoed this bill, but Congress overrode his veto. Because we have a system of checks and balances, one branch of government is able to check the other branches.

Easy Lesson

The president commands the armed forces, but Congress has the power to pay for the armed forces and declare war. Because of our system of three branches of government and our system of checks and balances, one branch of government is able to check the power of the other branches.

Easy Answer!

The Commander in Chief of the military is the President.

Q. 33	A. 33
Who signs bills to become laws?	• *the President*

Official USCIS Civics lesson

Every law begins as a proposal made by a member of Congress, either a senator (member of the Senate) or representative (member of the House of Representatives). When the Senate or House begins to debate the proposal, it is called a "bill." After debate in both houses of Congress, if a majority of both the Senate and House vote to pass the bill, it goes to the president. If the president wants the bill to become law, he signs it. If the president does not want the bill to become law, he vetoes it. The president cannot introduce a bill. If he has an idea for a bill, he must ask a member of Congress to introduce it.

Easy **Lesson**

If the president wants the bill to become law, he signs it. If the president does not want the bill to become law, he vetoes it.

Easy Answer!

The President signs bills to become law.

Q. 34	A. 34
Who vetoes bills?	• *the President*

Official USCIS Civics lesson

The president has veto power. This means that the president can reject a bill passed by Congress. If the president vetoes a bill, he prevents it from becoming a law. The president can send the bill back to Congress unsigned. Often he will list reasons why he rejects it. The president has 10 days to evaluate the bill. If the president does not sign the bill after 10 days and Congress is in session, the bill automatically becomes a law. If the president does nothing with the bill and Congress adjourns within the 10-day period, the bill does not become law—this is called a "pocket veto." If two-thirds of the House and two-thirds of the Senate vote to pass the bill again, the bill becomes a law, even though the president did not sign it. This process is called "overriding the president's veto." It is not easy to do.

Easy **Lesson**

The president can reject a bill passed by Congress. If the president vetoes a bill, he prevents it from becoming a law. If two-thirds of the House and two-thirds of the Senate vote to pass the bill again, the bill becomes a law, even though the president did not sign it.

Easy Answer!

The President vetoes bills.

Q. 35	A. 35
What does the President's Cabinet do?	• *advises the President*

Official USCIS Civics lesson

The Constitution says that the leaders of the executive departments should advise the president. These department leaders, most of them called "secretaries," make up the cabinet. The president nominates the cabinet members to be his advisors. For a nominee to be confirmed, a majority of the Senate must approve the nominee. Throughout history, presidents have been able to change who makes up the cabinet or add departments to the cabinet. For example, when the Department of Homeland Security was created, President George W. Bush added the leader of this department to his cabinet.

Easy **Lesson**

The Constitution says that the leaders of the executive departments should advise the president. These department leaders, most of them called "secretaries," make up the cabinet.

Easy Answer!

The President's Cabinet advises the President.

Q. 36	A. 36: *Secretary of Defense, Secretary of Education, Secretary of Energy, Secretary of Health and Human Services, Secretary of Homeland Security, Secretary of Housing and Urban Development, Secretary of Interior, Secretary of Labor, Secretary of State, Secretary of Transportation, Secretary of the Treasury, Secretary of Veterans Affairs, Attorney General, Vice President*
What are <u>two</u> Cabinet-level positions?	

Official USCIS Civics lesson

The people on the president's cabinet are the vice president and the heads of the 15 executive departments. The president may appoint other government officials to the cabinet. When George Washington was president, there were only four cabinet members: the secretary of state, secretary of the treasury, secretary of war, and attorney general. The government established the other executive departments later.

Easy **Lesson**

The people on the president's cabinet are the vice president and the heads of the 15 executive departments.

Easy Answer!

Two Cabinet-level positions are the Vice President and Secretary of State.

Q. 37	A. 37
What does the judicial branch do?	• *reviews laws* • *explains laws* • *resolves disputes (disagreements)* • *decides if a law goes against the Constitution*

Official USCIS Civics lesson

The judicial branch is one of the three branches of government. The Constitution established the judicial branch of government with the creation of the Supreme Court. Congress created the other federal courts. All these courts together make up the judicial branch. The courts review and explain the laws, and they resolve disagreements about the meaning of the law. The U.S. Supreme Court makes sure that laws are consistent with the Constitution. If a law is not consistent with the Constitution, the Court can declare it unconstitutional. In this case, the Court rejects the law. The Supreme Court makes the final decision about all cases that have to do with federal laws and treaties. It also rules on other cases, such as disagreements between states.

Easy Lesson

The judicial branch is one of the three branches of government. The Constitution established the judicial branch of government with the creation of the Supreme Court. Congress created the other federal courts. The courts review and explain the laws, and they resolve disagreements about the meaning of the law. The Supreme Court also rules on other cases, such as disagreements between states.

Easy Answer!

The judicial branch reviews laws.

Q. 38	A. 38
What is the highest court in the United States?	• *the Supreme Court*

Official USCIS Civics lesson

The U.S. Supreme Court has complete authority over all federal courts. Its rulings have a significant effect. A Supreme Court ruling can affect the outcome of many cases in the lower courts. The Supreme Court's interpretations of federal laws and of the Constitution are final. The Supreme Court is limited in its power over the states. It cannot make decisions about state law or state constitutions. The Court can decide that a state law or action conflicts with federal law or with the U.S. Constitution. If this happens, the state law becomes invalid. The Supreme Court case ruling Marbury v. Madison established this power, known as "judicial review." The Supreme Court also rules on cases about significant social and public policy issues that affect all Americans. The Supreme Court ruled on the court case Brown v. the Board of Education of Topeka, which ended racial segregation in schools.

Easy Lesson

The U.S. Supreme Court has complete authority over all federal courts. The Supreme Court's interpretations of federal laws and of the Constitution are final. However, it cannot make decisions about state law or state constitutions unless a state law or action conflicts with federal law or with the U.S. Constitution. The Supreme Court also rules on cases about significant social and public policy issues that affect all Americans.

Easy Answer!

The highest court in the United States is the Supreme Court.

Q. 39	A. 39
How many justices are on the Supreme Court?	• *nine (9)*

Official USCIS Civics lesson

The Constitution does not establish the number of justices on the Supreme Court. In the past, there have been as many as 10 and as few as six justices. Now, there are nine justices on the Supreme Court: eight associate justices and one chief justice. The Constitution gives the president the power to nominate justices to the Supreme Court. The nominee must then be confirmed by the Senate. Justices serve on the court for life or until they retire. For more information on the Supreme Court, go to www.supremecourt.gov.

Easy **Lesson**

The Constitution gives the president the power to nominate justices to the Supreme Court. The nominee must then be confirmed by the Senate. Justices serve on the court for life or until they retire. For more information on the Supreme Court, go to www.supremecourt.gov.

Easy Answer!

There are nine justices on the Supreme Court.

U.S. Supreme Court Building (6)

Q. 40	A. 40
Who is the Chief Justice of the United States now?	• *John Roberts* • *(John G. Roberts, Jr.)*

Official USCIS Civics lesson

John G. Roberts, Jr. is the 17th chief justice of the United States. After the death of former chief justice William Rehnquist in September 2005, President George W. Bush nominated Roberts for this position. Judge Roberts became chief justice when he was 50. He is the youngest chief justice since 1801, when John Marshall became chief justice at the age of 45. Before he became chief justice, Judge Roberts served on the U.S. Court of Appeals for the District of Columbia Circuit. Although the chief justice of the United States is the highest official in the judicial branch, his vote on the Supreme Court carries the same weight as the other justices.

Easy Lesson

John G. Roberts, Jr. is the 17th chief justice of the United States. Judge Roberts became chief justice when he was 50.

Easy Answer!

The Chief Justice of the United States now is John Roberts.

Q. 41	A. 41
Under our Constitution, some powers belong to the federal government. What is <u>one</u> power of the federal government?	• *to print money* • *to declare war* • *to create an army* • *to make treaties*

Official USCIS Civics lesson

The powers of government are divided between the federal government and the state governments. The federal government is known as a limited government. Its powers are restricted to those described in the U.S. Constitution. The Constitution gives the federal government the power to print money, declare war, create an army, and make treaties with other nations. Most other powers that are not given to the federal government in the Constitution belong to the states.

Easy **Lesson**

The powers of government are divided between the federal government and the state governments. The Constitution gives the federal government the power to print money, declare war, create an army, and make treaties with other nations. Most other powers that are not given to the federal government in the Constitution belong to the states.

Easy Answer!

One power of the federal government is to declare war.

Q. 42	A. 42
Under our Constitution, some powers belong to the states. What is <u>one</u> power of the states?	• *provide schooling and education* • *provide protection (police)* • *provide safety (fire departments)* • *give a driver's license* • *approve zoning and land use*

Official USCIS Civics lesson

In the United States, the federal and state governments both hold power. Before the Constitution, the 13 colonies governed themselves individually much like state governments. It was not until the Articles of Confederation and then the Constitution that a national or federal government was established. Today, although each state has its own constitution, these state constitutions cannot conflict with the U.S. Constitution. The U.S. Constitution is the supreme law of the land. The state governments hold powers not given to the federal government in the U.S. Constitution. Some powers of the state government are the power to create traffic regulations and marriage requirements, and to issue driver's licenses. The Constitution also provides a list of powers that the states do not have. For example, states cannot coin (create) money. The state and federal governments also share some powers, such as the ability to tax people.

Easy **Lesson**

Although each state has its own constitution, the state constitutions cannot conflict with the U.S. Constitution. The state governments hold powers not given to the federal government in the U.S. Constitution. Some powers of the state government are the power to create traffic regulations and issue driver's licenses. The Constitution also provides a list of powers that the states do not have. For example, states cannot coin (create) money. The state and federal governments also share some powers, such as the ability to tax people.

Easy Answer!

One power of the states is to give a driver's license.

Q. 43	A. 43
Who is the Governor of your state now?	**Answers will vary. [District of Columbia residents should answer that D.C. does not have a Governor.] Visit usa.gov/states-and-territories to find the Governor of your state.**

Official USCIS Civics lesson

To learn the name of the governor of your state or territory, go to *www.usa.gov*
Similar to the federal government, most states have three branches of government. The branches are executive, legislative, and judicial. The governor is the chief executive of the state. The governor's job in a state government is similar to the president's job in the federal government. However, the state laws that a governor carries out are different from the federal laws that the president carries out. The Constitution says that certain issues are covered by federal, not state, laws. All other issues are covered by state laws. The governor's duties and powers vary from state to state. The number of years that a governor is elected to serve—called a "term"—is four years. The exceptions are New Hampshire and Vermont, where governors serve for two years.

Easy Lesson

(The names of Governors are on page 155.)

The governor's job in a state government is similar to the president's job in the federal government. The governor's duties and powers vary from state to state. The number of years that a governor is elected to serve—called a "term"—is four years. The exceptions are New Hampshire and Vermont, where governors serve for two years.

Easy Answer!

The name of the governor of my state is _____.

Q. 44	A. 44
What is the capital of your state?*	*Answers will vary.* *[District of Columbia residents should answer that D.C. is not a state and does not have a capital. Residents of U.S. territories should name the capital of the territory.]*

Official USCIS Civics lesson

To learn the capital of your state or territory, go to www.usa.gov. Each state or territory has its own capital. The state capital is where the state government conducts its business. It is similar to the nation's capital, Washington, D.C., where the federal government conducts its business. Some state capitals have moved from one city to another over the years, but the state capitals have not changed since 1910. Usually, the governor lives in the state's capital city.

Easy **Lesson**

(The state capitals are listed on page 154.)

Each state or territory has its own capital. The state capital is where the state government conducts its business. Usually, the governor lives in the state's capital city.

Easy Answer!

The capital of my state is _____.

Q. 45	A. 45
What are the <u>two</u> major political parties in the United States?*	• *Democratic and Republican*

Official USCIS Civics lesson

_____

The Constitution did not establish political parties. President George Washington specifically warned against them. But early in U.S. history, two political groups developed. They were the Democratic Republicans and the Federalists. Today, the two major political parties are the Democratic Party and the Republican Party. President Andrew Jackson created the Democratic Party from the Democratic Republicans. The Republican Party took over from the Whigs as a major party in the 1860s. The first Republican president was Abraham Lincoln. Throughout U.S. history, there have been other parties. These parties have included the Know-Nothing (also called American Party), Bull-Moose (also called Progressive), Reform, and Green parties. They have played various roles in American politics. Political party membership in the United States is voluntary. Parties are made up of people who organize to promote their candidates for election and to promote their views about public policies.

Easy **Lesson**

_____

Today, the two major political parties are the Democratic Party and the Republican Party. Throughout U.S. history, there have been other parties. Political party membership in the United States is voluntary. Parties are made up of people who organize to promote their candidates for election and to promote their views about public policies.

Easy Answer!

_____

The two major political parties in the United States are the Democratic and Republican parties.

Q. 46	A. 46
What is the political party of the President now?	• *Republican (Party)*

Official USCIS Civics lesson

Visit uscis.gov/citizenship/testupdates for the political party of the President.

Easy **Lesson**

     The current president, Donald Trump, is a member of the Republican Party. The Republican Party is also known as the "Grand Old Party" or the "GOP."

Easy Answer!

The political party of the President now is the Republican Party.

Q. 47	A. 47
What is the name of the Speaker of the House of Representatives now?	• *Nancy Pelosi*

Official USCIS Civics lesson

Visit uscis.gov/citizenship/testupdates for the name of the Speaker of the House of Representatives. For more information on the speaker of the House of Representatives, visit house.gov.

Easy **Lesson**

The current Speaker of the House of Representatives is Nancy Pelosi. The speaker is second in line to the succession of the presidency after the vice president.

Easy Answer!

The name of the Speaker of the House of Representatives now is Nancy Pelosi.

Q. 48	A. 48
There are four amendments to the Constitution about who can vote. Describe <u>one</u> of them.	• *Citizens eighteen (18) and older (can vote).* • *You don't have to pay (a poll tax) to vote.* • *Any citizen can vote. (Women and men can vote.)* • *A male citizen of any race (can vote).*

Official USCIS Civics lesson

Voting is one of the most important civic responsibilities of citizens in the United States. In a democratic society, the people choose the leaders who will represent them. There are four amendments to the Constitution about voting. The 15th Amendment permits American men of all races to vote. It was written after the Civil War and the end of slavery. The 19th Amendment gave women the right to vote. It resulted from the women's suffrage movement (the women's rights movement). After the 15th Amendment was passed, some leaders of the southern states were upset that African Americans could vote. These leaders designed fees called poll taxes to stop them from voting. The 24th Amendment made these poll taxes illegal. The 26th Amendment lowered the voting age from 21 to 18.

Easy **Lesson**

There are four amendments to the Constitution about voting.

1) The 15th Amendment permits American men of all races to vote.

2) The 19th Amendment gave women the right to vote.

3) The 24th Amendment made poll taxes (taxes to be allowed to vote) illegal.

4) The 26th Amendment lowered the voting age from 21 to 18.

Easy Answer!

The 26th Amendment lowered the voting age from 21 to 18.

Q. 49	A. 49
What is <u>one</u> responsibility that is only for United States citizens?*	• *serve on a jury* • *vote in a federal election*

Official USCIS Civics lesson

Two responsibilities of U.S. citizens are to serve on a jury and vote in federal elections. The Constitution gives citizens the right to a trial by a jury. The jury is made up of U.S. citizens. Participation of citizens on a jury helps ensure a fair trial. Another important responsibility of citizens is voting. The law does not require citizens to vote, but voting is a very important part of any democracy. By voting, citizens are participating in the democratic process. Citizens vote for leaders to represent them and their ideas, and the leaders support the citizens' interests.

Easy **Lesson**

Two responsibilities of U.S. citizens are to serve on a jury and vote in federal elections. Participation of citizens on a jury helps ensure a fair trial. Another important responsibility of citizens is voting. By voting, citizens are participating in the democratic process.

Easy Answer!

One responsibility that is only for U.S. citizens is to vote in a federal election.

Q. 50	A. 50
Name <u>one</u> right only for United States citizens.	• *vote in a federal election* • *run for federal office*

Official USCIS Civics lesson

U.S. citizens have the right to vote in federal elections. Permanent residents can vote in local or state elections that do not require voters to be U.S. citizens. Only U.S. citizens can vote in federal elections. U.S. citizens can also run for federal office. Qualifications to run for the Senate or House of Representatives include being a U.S. citizen for a certain number of years. A candidate for Senate must be a U.S. citizen for at least 9 years. A candidate for the House must be a U.S. citizen for at least 7 years. To run for president of the United States, a candidate must be a native-born (not naturalized) citizen. In addition to the benefits of citizenship, U.S. citizens have certain responsibilities—to respect the law, stay informed on issues, participate in the democratic process, and pay their taxes.

***Easy* Lesson**

U.S. citizens have the right to vote in federal elections and also run for a federal office. Only U.S. citizens can vote in federal elections.

Easy Answer!

One right that is only for United States citizens is the right to vote in a federal election.

Q. 51	A. 51
What are <u>two</u> rights of everyone living in the United States?	• *freedom of expression* • *freedom of speech* • *freedom of assembly* • *freedom to petition the government* • *freedom of worship* • *the right to bear arms*

Official USCIS Civics lesson

Thomas Jefferson said, "[The] best principles [of our republic] secure to all its citizens a perfect equality of rights." Millions of immigrants have come to America to have these rights. The Constitution and the Bill of Rights give many of these rights to all people living in the United States. These rights include the freedom of expression, of religion, of speech, and the right to bear arms. All people living in the United States also have many of the same duties as citizens, such as paying taxes and obeying the laws.

Easy Lesson

The Constitution and the Bill of Rights give many of these rights to all people living in the United States. Those rights include freedom of expression, of religion, of speech, freedom of assembly (freedom to meet together), freedom to petition the government (ask the government for something), freedom of worship, and the right to bear arms (own weapons).

Easy Answer!

Two rights of everyone living in the United States are freedom of speech and freedom of worship.

Q. 52	A. 52
What do we show loyalty to when we say the Pledge of Allegiance?	• *the United States* • *the flag*

Official USCIS Civics lesson

The flag is an important symbol of the United States. The Pledge of Allegiance to the flag states, "I pledge allegiance to the Flag of the United States of America and to the Republic for which it stands, one Nation, under God, indivisible, with liberty and justice for all." When we say the Pledge of Allegiance, we usually stand facing the flag with the right hand over the heart. Francis Bellamy wrote the pledge. It was first published in The Youth's Companion magazine in 1892 for children to say on the anniversary of Columbus's discovery of America. Congress officially recognized the pledge on June 22, 1942. Two changes have been made since it was written in 1892. "I pledge allegiance to my flag" was changed to "I pledge allegiance to the Flag of the United States of America." Congress added the phrase "under God" on June 14, 1954.

***Easy* Lesson**

The flag is an important symbol of the United States. When we recite the Pledge of Allegiance to the flag, we usually stand facing the flag with the right hand over the heart.

Easy Answer!

When we say the Pledge of Allegiance, we show loyalty to the United States.

Q. 53	A. 53
What is <u>one</u> promise you make when you become a United States citizen?	• *give up loyalty to other countries* • *defend the Constitution and laws of United States* • *obey the laws of the United States* • *serve in the U.S. military (if needed)* • *serve (do important work for) the nation (if needed)* • *be loyal to the United States*

Official USCIS Civics lesson

When the United States became an independent country, the Constitution gave Congress the power to establish a uniform rule of naturalization. Congress made rules about how immigrants could become citizens. Many of these requirements are still valid today, such as the requirements to live in the United States for a specific period of time, to be of good moral character, and to understand and support the principles of the Constitution. After an immigrant fulfills all of the requirements to become a U.S. citizen, the final step is to take an Oath of Allegiance at a naturalization ceremony. The Oath of Allegiance states, "I hereby declare, on oath, that I absolutely and entirely renounce and abjure all allegiance and fidelity to any foreign prince, potentate, state, or sovereignty of whom or which I have heretofore been a subject or citizen; that I will support and defend the Constitution and laws of the United States of America against all enemies, foreign and domestic; that I will bear true faith and allegiance to the same; that I will bear arms on behalf of the United States when required by the law; that I will perform noncombatant service in the Armed Forces of the United States when required by the law; that I will perform work of national importance under civilian direction when required by the law; and that I take this obligation freely without any mental reservation or purpose of evasion; so help me God."

Easy Answer!

One promise you make when you become a citizen is to obey the laws of the United States.

Q. 54	A. 54
How old do citizens have to be to vote for President?*	• *eighteen (18) and older*

Official USCIS Civics lesson

For most of U.S. history, Americans had to be at least 21 years old to vote. At the time of the Vietnam War, during the 1960s and 1970s, many people thought that people who were old enough to fight in a war should also be old enough to vote. In 1971, the 26th Amendment changed the minimum voting age from 21 to 18 for all federal, state, and local elections. The National Voter Registration Act of 1993 made it easier for people to register to vote. Now they can register to vote by mail, at public assistance offices, or when they apply for or renew their driver's license.

Easy Lesson

In 1971, the 26th Amendment changed the minimum voting age from 21 to 18 for all federal, state, and local elections.

Easy Answer!

Citizens have to be eighteen or older to vote for President.

Q. 55	A. 55
What are <u>two</u> ways that Americans can participate in their democracy?	• *vote* • *join a political party* • *help with a campaign* • *join a civic group* • *join a community group* • *give an elected official your opinion on an issue* • *call Senators and Representatives* • *publicly support or oppose an issue or policy* • *run for office, and* • *write to a newspaper*

Official USCIS Civics lesson

Citizens play an active part in their communities. When Americans engage in the political process, democracy stays alive and strong. There are many ways for people to be involved. They can volunteer to help new immigrants learn English and civics, join the Parent Teacher Association (PTA) of their child's school, run for a position on the local school board, or volunteer to help at a polling station. People can also vote, help with a political campaign, join a civic or community organization, or call their senator or representative about an issue that is important to them.

***Easy* Lesson**

Citizens play an active part in their communities. When Americans engage in the political process, democracy stays alive and strong. There are many ways for people to be involved.

Easy Answer!

Two ways that Americans can participate in their democracy is to vote and by joining a political party.

Q. 56	A. 56
When is the last day you can send in federal income tax forms?*	• *April 15*

Official USCIS Civics lesson

The last day to send in your federal income tax to the Internal Revenue Service is April 15 of each year. The Constitution gave the federal government the power to collect taxes. The federal government needs money to pay the nation's debts and to defend and provide for the needs of the country. When the country was young, it was difficult to raise money from the 13 original states. The government began collecting income tax for the first time through the Revenue Act of 1861. This was only temporary. In 1894, a flat rate federal income tax was enacted, but the Supreme Court said this was unconstitutional. Finally, in 1913, the 16th Amendment was ratified. It gave Congress the power to collect income taxes. Today, "taxable income" is money that is earned from wages, self-employment, tips, and the sale of property. The government uses these taxes to keep our country safe and secure. It also tries to cure and prevent diseases through research. In addition, the government protects our money in banks by insuring it, educates children and adults, and builds and repairs our roads and highways. Taxes are used to do these things and many more.

***Easy* Lesson**

The last day to send in your federal income tax to the Internal Revenue Service is April 15 of each year. The government uses these taxes to keep our country safe and secure. It also provides many benefits.

Easy Answer!

The last day that you can send in federal tax returns is April 15.

Q. 57	A. 57
When must all men register for the Selective Service?	• *at age eighteen (18)* • *between eighteen (18) and twenty-six (26)*

Official USCIS Civics lesson

President Lincoln tried to draft men to fight during the Civil War, but many people became angry and rioted. In 1917, Congress passed the Selective Service Act. This act gave President Woodrow Wilson the power to temporarily increase the U.S. military during World War I. In 1940, President Franklin Roosevelt signed the Selective Training and Service Act, which created the first draft during peacetime. This was the beginning of the Selective Service System in the United States today. The draft was needed again for the Korean and Vietnam Wars. Today, there is no draft, but all men between 18 and 26 years old must register with the Selective Service System. When a man registers, he tells the government that he is available to serve in the U.S. Armed Forces. He can register at a United States post office or on the Internet. To register for Selective Service on the Internet, visit the Selective Service website at www.sss.gov.

Easy Lesson

Although today there is no draft, all men between 18 and 26 years old must register with the Selective Service System. When a man registers, he tells the government that he is available to serve in the U.S. Armed Forces.

Easy Answer!

All men must register with the Selective Service System at age eighteen.

Q. 58	A. 58
What is <u>one</u> reason colonists came to America?	• *freedom* • *political liberty* • *religious freedom* • *economic opportunity* • *practice their religion* • *escape persecution*

Official USCIS Civics lesson

In the 1600s and 1700s, colonists from England and other European countries sailed across the Atlantic Ocean to the American colonies. Some left Europe to escape religious restrictions or persecution, to practice their religion freely. Many came for political freedom, and some came for economic opportunity. These freedoms and opportunities often did not exist in the colonists' home countries. For these settlers, the American colonies were a chance for freedom and a new life. Today, many people come to the United States for these same reasons.

***Easy* Lesson**

In the 1600s and 1700s, colonists from England and other European countries sailed across the Atlantic Ocean to the American colonies. For these settlers, the American colonies were a chance for freedom and a new life. Today, many people come to the United States for these same reasons.

Easy Answer!

One reason colonists came to America was to have freedom.

Q. 59	A. 59
Who lived in America before the Europeans arrived?	• *American Indians* • *Native Americans*

Official USCIS Civics lesson

_____

Great American Indian tribes such as the Navajo, Sioux, Cherokee, and Iroquois lived in America at the time the Pilgrims arrived. The Pilgrims settled in an area where a tribe called the Wampanoag lived. The Wampanoag taught the Pilgrims important skills, such as how to farm with different methods and how to grow crops such as corn, beans, and squash. Relations with some American Indian tribes became tense and confrontational as more Europeans moved to America and migrated west. Eventually, after much violence, the settlers defeated those American Indian tribes and took much of their land.

Easy **Lesson**

_____

 Great American Indian tribes such as the Navajo, Sioux, Cherokee, and Iroquois lived in America at the time the Pilgrims arrived. Eventually, after much violence, the settlers defeated those American Indian tribes and took much of their land.

Easy Answer!

_____

American Indians lived in America before the Europeans arrived.

Q. 60	A. 60
What group of people was taken to America and sold as slaves?	• *Africans* • *people from Africa*

Official USCIS Civics lesson

Slavery existed in many countries long before America was founded. By 1700, many Africans were being brought to the American colonies as slaves. Men, women, and children were brought against their will. They were often separated from their families when they were sold as slaves. Slaves worked without payment and without basic rights. Most worked in agriculture, but slaves did many other kinds of work in the colonies, too. Slavery created a challenge for a nation founded on individual freedoms and democratic beliefs. It was one of the major causes of the American Civil War.

Easy **Lesson**

By 1700, many Africans were being brought to the American colonies as slaves. Slavery created a challenge for a nation founded on individual freedoms and democratic beliefs. It was one of the major causes of the American Civil War.

Easy Answer!

Africans were taken to America and sold as slaved.

Q. 61	A. 61
Why did the colonists fight the British?	• **because of high taxes (taxation without representation)** • **because the British army stayed in their houses (boarding, quartering)** • **because they didn't have self-government**

Official USCIS Civics lesson

The American colonists' anger had been growing for years before the Revolutionary War began in 1775. The decision to separate from the British was not an easy choice for many colonists. However, Great Britain's "repeated injuries" against the Americans, as noted in the Declaration of Independence, convinced many to join the rebellion. The British taxed the colonists without their consent, and the colonists had nobody to represent their needs and ideas to the British government. They were also angry because ordinary colonists were forced to let British soldiers sleep and eat in their homes. The colonists believed the British did not respect their basic rights. The British governed the colonists without their consent, denying them self-government.

Easy Lesson

Great Britain's "repeated injuries" against the Americans, as noted in the Declaration of Independence, convinced many to join the rebellion. The colonists believed the British did not respect their basic rights. The British governed the colonists without their consent, denying them self-government.

Easy Answer!

The colonists fought the British because they did not have self-government.

Q. 62	A. 62
Who wrote the Declaration of Independence?	• *(Thomas) Jefferson*

Official USCIS Civics lesson

Thomas Jefferson wrote the Declaration of Independence in 1776. He was a very important political leader and thinker. Some of the most important ideas about the American government are found in the Declaration of Independence, such as the idea that all people are created equal. Another important idea is that people are born with certain rights including life, liberty, and the pursuit of happiness. Jefferson was the third president of the United States, serving from 1801 to 1809. Before becoming president, Jefferson was governor of Virginia and the first U.S. secretary of state. He strongly supported individual rights, especially freedom of religion. Jefferson wanted to protect these rights. For this reason, he did not want a strong national government.

Easy Lesson

Thomas Jefferson wrote the Declaration of Independence in 1776. He was a very important political leader and thinker and third president of the United States.

Easy Answer!

Thomas Jefferson wrote the Declaration of Independence.

Thomas Jefferson (1)

Q. 63	A. 63
When was the Declaration of Independence adopted?	• *July 4, 1776*

Official USCIS Civics lesson

In 1774, representatives from 12 of the 13 colonies met in Philadelphia, Pennsylvania, for the First Continental Congress. Of the 13 colonies, only Georgia was absent. These representatives were angry about British laws that treated them unfairly. They began to organize an army. The Second Continental Congress met in 1775 after fighting began between the colonists and the British Army. This Congress asked Thomas Jefferson and others to write the Declaration of Independence. When Thomas Jefferson finished his draft of the Declaration of Independence, he took it to John Adams, Benjamin Franklin, and the others on the committee to review it. After changes were made by the committee, the Declaration was read to the members of the entire Congress. The purpose of the Declaration was to announce the separation of the colonies from England. The Declaration of Independence stated that if a government does not protect the rights of the people, the people can create a new government. For this reason, the colonists separated from their British rulers. On July 4, 1776, the Second Continental Congress adopted the Declaration of Independence.

Easy Lesson

(To "adopt" the Declaration of Independence means to accept the declaration as binding.) In 1774, representatives from 12 of the 13 colonies met in Philadelphia, Pennsylvania and wrote the Declaration of Independence. On July 4, 1776, the Second Continental Congress adopted the Declaration of Independence.

Easy Answer!

The Declaration of Independence was adopted on July 4, 1776.

Q. 64	A. 64
There were 13 original states. Name <u>three</u>.	• **New Hampshire • Massachusetts** • **Rhode Island • Connecticut** • **New York • New Jersey** • **Pennsylvania • Delaware** • **Maryland • Virginia • Georgia** • **North Carolina • South Carolina**

Official USCIS Civics lesson

The 13 original states were all former British colonies. Representatives from these colonies came together and declared independence from Great Britain in 1776. After the Revolutionary War, the colonies became free and independent states. When the 13 colonies became states, each state set up its own government. They wrote state constitutions. Eventually, the people in these states created a new form of national government that would unite all the states into a single nation under the U.S. Constitution. The first three colonies to become states were Delaware, Pennsylvania, and New Jersey. This happened in 1787. Eight colonies became states in 1788. These were Georgia, Connecticut, Massachusetts, Maryland, South Carolina, New Hampshire, Virginia, and New York. North Carolina became a state in 1789. Rhode Island became a state in 1790. Although the colonies were recognized as states after the Declaration of Independence, the date of statehood is based on when they ratified (accepted) the U.S. Constitution. Today, the United States has 50 states.

***Easy* Lesson**

The 13 original states were all former British colonies. Today, the United States has 50 states.

Easy Answer!

Three original colonies were New York, New Jersey, and New Hampshire.

13 Original Colonies (5)

(East coast, bordering Atlantic Ocean)

Q. 65	A. 65
What happened at the Constitutional Convention?	• *The Constitution was written.* • *The Founding Fathers wrote the Constitution.*

Official USCIS Civics lesson

The Constitutional Convention was held in Philadelphia, Pennsylvania, from May to September 1787. Fifty-five delegates from 12 of the original 13 states (except for Rhode Island) met to write amendments to the Articles of Confederation. The delegates met because many American leaders did not like the Articles. The national government under the Articles of Confederation was not strong enough. Instead of changing the Articles of Confederation, the delegates decided to create a new governing document with a stronger national government—the Constitution. Each state sent delegates, who worked for four months in secret to allow for free and open discussion as they wrote the new document. The delegates who attended the Constitutional Convention are called "the Framers." On September 17, 1787, 39 of the delegates signed the new Constitution.

***Easy* Lesson**

From May to September 1787, fifty-five delegates from 12 of the original 13 states (except for Rhode Island) met and created the Constitution which set up the new American government.

Easy Answer!

Constitutional Convention (1)

At the Constitutional Convention, the Constitution was written.

Q. 66	A. 66
When was the Constitution written?	• *1787*

Official USCIS Civics lesson

The Constitution, written in 1787, created a new system of U.S. government—the same system we have today. James Madison was the main writer of the Constitution. He became the fourth president of the United States. The U.S. Constitution is short, but it defines the principles of government and the rights of citizens in the United States. The document has a preamble and seven articles. Since its adoption, the Constitution has been amended (changed) 27 times. Three-fourths of the states (9 of the original 13) were required to ratify (approve) the Constitution. Delaware was the first state to ratify the Constitution on December 7, 1787. In 1788, New Hampshire was the ninth state to ratify the Constitution. On March 4, 1789, the Constitution took effect and Congress met for the first time. George Washington was inaugurated as president the same year. By 1790, all 13 states had ratified the Constitution.

Easy Lesson

The Constitution, written in 1787, created a new system of U.S. government—the same system we have today. By 1790, all 13 states had ratified the Constitution.

Easy Answer!

The Constitution was written in 1787.

Q. 67	A. 67
The Federalist Papers supported the passage of the U.S. Constitution. Name <u>one</u> of the writers.	• *(James) Madison* • *(Alexander) Hamilton* • *(John) Jay* • *Publius*

Official USCIS Civics lesson

The Federalist Papers were 85 essays that were printed in New York newspapers while New York State was deciding whether or not to support the U.S. Constitution. The essays were written in 1787 and 1788 by Alexander Hamilton, John Jay, and James Madison under the pen name "Publius." The essays explained why the state should ratify the Constitution. Other newspapers outside New York also published the essays as other states were deciding to ratify the Constitution. In 1788, the papers were published together in a book called The Federalist. Today, people still read the Federalist Papers to help them understand the Constitution.

***Easy* Lesson**

The Federalist Papers were 85 essays that were printed in New York newspapers while New York State was deciding whether or not to support the U.S. Constitution. The essays were written in 1787 and 1788.

Easy Answer!

One of the writers of the Federalist Papers was John Jay.

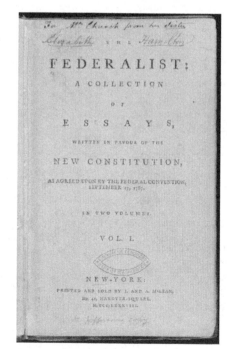

Cover Page Federalist Papers (13)

Q. 68	A. 68
What is <u>one</u> thing Benjamin Franklin is famous for?	• **oldest member of Constitutional Convention** • **first Postmaster General of the United States** • **writer of "Poor Richard's Almanac"** • **started the first free libraries**

Official USCIS Civics lesson

Benjamin Franklin was one of the most influential Founding Fathers of the United States. He was the oldest delegate to the Constitutional Convention and one of the signers of the U.S. Constitution. He was a printer, author, politician, diplomat, and inventor. By his mid-20s, he was an accomplished printer, and he began writing books and papers. Franklin's most famous publication was Poor Richard's Almanac. He also organized America's first library. Its members loaned books to one another. He was very active in colonial politics. He also visited England and France many times as a U.S. diplomat. In 1775, the Second Continental Congress appointed Franklin the first postmaster general.

Easy **Lesson**

Benjamin Franklin was one of the most influential Founding Fathers of the United States. He was the oldest delegate to the Constitutional Convention and one of the signers of the U.S. Constitution.

Easy Answer!

One thing Benjamin Franklin is famous for is starting free libraries.

Benjamin Franklin (10)

Q. 69	A. 69
Who is the "Father of Our Country"?	• *(George) Washington*

Official USCIS Civics lesson

George Washington is called the Father of Our Country. He was the first American president. Before that, he was a brave general who led the Continental Army to victory over Great Britain during the American Revolutionary War. After his victory over the British Army, Washington retired to his farm in Virginia named Mount Vernon. He left retirement to help create the new country's system of government. He presided over the Constitutional Convention in Philadelphia in 1787.

Easy Lesson

George Washington is called the Father of Our Country. He was the first American president. He presided over the Constitutional Convention in Philadelphia in 1787.

Easy Answer!

The father of Our Country is George Washington.

George Washington (11)

Q. 70	A. 70
Who was the first President?*	• *(George) Washington*

Official USCIS Civics lesson

George Washington was the first president of the United States. He began his first term in 1789. He served for a second term beginning in 1793. Washington played an important role in forming the new nation and encouraged Americans to unite. He also helped define the American presidency. He voluntarily resigned from the presidency after two terms. He set an example for future leaders in his own country and the world by voluntarily giving up power. The tradition of a president serving no more than two terms continued in the United States until Franklin D. Roosevelt, who was elected to office four times (1933–1945). The 22nd Amendment to the Constitution, passed in 1947, now limits presidents to two terms.

***Easy* Lesson**

George Washington was the first president of the United States. He began his first term in 1789. He served for a second term beginning in 1793.

Easy Answer!

The first President was George Washington.

Q. 71	A. 71
What territory did the United States buy from France in 1803?	• *the Louisiana Territory* • *Louisiana*

Official USCIS Civics lesson

The Louisiana Territory was a large area west of the Mississippi River. It was 828,000 square miles. In 1803, the United States bought the Louisiana Territory from France for $15 million. The Louisiana Purchase Treaty was signed in Paris on April 30, 1803. It was the largest acquisition of land in American history. Farmers could now ship their farm products down the Mississippi River without permission from other countries. This was important because the city of New Orleans was a major shipping port. The Louisiana Purchase doubled the size of the United States and expanded it westward. Meriwether Lewis and William Clark led an expedition to map the Louisiana Territory.

Easy **Lesson**

In 1803, the United States bought the Louisiana Territory from France for $15 million. The Louisiana Purchase doubled the size of the United States and expanded it westward.

Easy Answer!

The name of the territory that the United States bought from France in 1803 is the Louisiana Territory.

Q. 72	A. 72
Name one war fought by the United States in the 1800s.	• **War of 1812** • **Mexican-American War** • **Civil War** • **Spanish-American War**

Official USCIS Civics lesson

The United States fought four major wars in the 1800s - the War of 1812, the Mexican-American War, the Civil War, and the Spanish-American War. The War of 1812 lasted from 1812 through 1815. President James Madison asked Congress to declare war on Great Britain. The British were stopping and seizing American ships. They were also arming American Indians to fight against the Americans. As a result of this war, the nation's trade was disrupted and the U.S. Capitol was burned. The Americans won the war. This was the first time after the Revolutionary War that America had to fight a foreign country to protect its independence. The Mexican-American War was a conflict between Mexico and America. The war began in Texas in 1846. President James Polk ordered General Zachary Taylor and his forces to occupy land claimed by both the United States and Mexico. President Polk believed westward expansion was important for the United States to grow. When Mexico attacked, the United States went to war with Mexico. When the war ended in February 1848, the United States and Mexico signed the Treaty of Guadalupe Hidalgo. This treaty gave Texas to the United States and extended the boundaries of the United States west to the Pacific Ocean. In the Civil War, the people of the United States fought against each other. Americans in the northern states fought to support the federal government ("the Union") against Americans from the southern states. The southern states were trying to separate themselves to form a new nation, the Confederate States of America ("the Confederacy"). The war lasted from 1861 to 1865, when the Confederate army surrendered to the Union army. Many lives were lost in the American Civil War. In 1898, the United States fought Spain in the Spanish American War. The United States wanted to help Cuba become independent from Spain because the United States had economic interests in Cuba. The war began when a U.S. battleship was sunk near Cuba. Many Americans believed it was the Spanish who attacked the ship. For this reason, America went to war with Spain. By the end of 1898, the war was over with a victory for the United States. Cuba had its independence, and Guam, Puerto Rico, and the Philippines became territories of the United States.

***Easy* Lesson**

_____

The United States fought four major wars in the 1800s (the War of 1812, the Mexican-American War, the Civil War, and the Spanish-American War.

Easy Answer!

_____

One of the wars fought by the United States in the 1800s was the Civil War.

Civil War Battle (7)

Q. 73	A. 73
Name the U.S. war between the North and the South.	• *the Civil War* • *the War between the States*

Official USCIS Civics lesson

The American Civil War is also known as the War between the States. It was a war between the people in the northern states and those in the southern states. The Civil War was fought in many places across the United States, but most battles were fought in the southern states. The first battle was at Fort Sumter, South Carolina. The first major battle between the northern (Union) army and the southern (Confederate) army took place at Bull Run, in Manassas, Virginia, in July 1861. The Union expected the war to end quickly. After its defeat at the Battle of Bull Run, the Union realized that the war would be long and difficult. In 1865, the Civil War ended with the capture of the Confederate capital in Richmond, Virginia. Confederate General Robert E. Lee surrendered to Lt. General Ulysses S. Grant of the Union army at Appomattox Courthouse in central Virginia. Over the four-year period, more than 3 million Americans fought in the Civil War and more than 600,000 people died.

***Easy* Lesson**

The American Civil War is also known as the War between the States. It was a war between the people in the northern states and those in the southern states. Over the four-year period, more than 3 million Americans fought in the Civil War and more than 600,000 people died.

Easy Answer!

The name of the U.S. war between the North and the South is the Civil War.

Q. 74	A. 74
Name <u>one</u> problem that led to the Civil War.	• *slavery* •*economic reasons* •*states' rights*

Official USCIS Civics lesson

The Civil War began when 11 southern states voted to secede (separate) from the United States to form their own country, the Confederate States of America. These southern states believed that the federal government of the United States threatened their right to make their own decisions. They wanted states' rights with each state making their own decisions about their government. If the national government contradicted the state, they did not want to follow the national government. The North and South had very different economic systems. The South's agriculture based economy depended heavily on slave labor. The southern states feared that the United States government would end slavery. The southern states believed that this would hurt their economic and political independence. The economy of the northern states was more industrial and did not depend on slavery. The northern states fought to keep all the United States together in "the Union." They tried to stop the southern states from separating into a new Confederate nation. There were also many people in the North who wanted to end slavery. These differences led to the American Civil War, which lasted from 1861 until 1865.

Easy Lesson

The Civil War lasted from 1861 to 1865. The problems that led to the Civil War were slavery, economic reasons and states' rights.

Easy Answer!

One problem that led to the Civil War was slavery.

Q. 75	A. 75
What was <u>one</u> important thing that Abraham Lincoln did?*	• **freed the slaves (Emancipation Proclamation)** • **saved (or preserved) the Union** • **led the United States during the Civil War**

Official USCIS Civics lesson

Abraham Lincoln was president of the United States from 1861 to 1865, and led the nation during the Civil War. Lincoln thought the separation of the southern (Confederate) states was unconstitutional, and he wanted to preserve the Union. In 1863, during the Civil War, he issued the Emancipation Proclamation. It declared that the slaves who lived in the rebelling Confederate states were forever free. Lincoln is also famous for his "Gettysburg Address." He gave that speech at Gettysburg, Pennsylvania, in November 1863. Earlier that year, at the Battle of Gettysburg, the northern (Union) army had won a major battle to stop the Confederate army from invading the North. To honor the many who died in this battle, the governor of Pennsylvania established the Soldiers' National Cemetery at Gettysburg. Lincoln spoke at the dedication ceremony and praised those who fought and died in battle. He asked those still living to rededicate themselves to saving the Union so that "government of the people, by the people, for the people shall not perish from the earth." On April 14, 1865, soon after taking office for his second term, Abraham Lincoln was killed by a southern supporter, John Wilkes Booth, at Ford's Theatre in Washington, D.C.

***Easy* Lesson**

Abraham Lincoln was president of the United States from 1861 to 1865, and led the nation during the Civil War.

Easy Answer!

One important thing Abraham Lincoln did was that he freed the slaves.

Abraham Lincoln (1)

Q. 76	A. 76
What did the Emancipation Proclamation do?	• *freed the slaves* • *freed slaves in the Confederacy* • *freed slaves in the Confederate states* • *freed slaves in most Southern states*

Official USCIS Civics lesson

In 1863, in the middle of the Civil War, President Abraham Lincoln issued the Emancipation Proclamation. The Emancipation Proclamation declared that slaves living in the southern or Confederate states were free. Many slaves joined the Union army. In 1865, the Civil War ended and the southern slaves kept their right to be free. The Emancipation Proclamation led to the 13th Amendment to the Constitution, which ended slavery in all of the United States.

Easy Lesson

In 1863, in the middle of the Civil War, President Abraham Lincoln issued the Emancipation Proclamation. It declared that slaves living in the southern or Confederate states were free. The Emancipation Proclamation led to the 13th Amendment to the Constitution, which ended slavery in all of the United States.

Easy Answer!

The Emancipation Proclamation freed the slaves.

Q. 77	A. 77
What did Susan B. Anthony do?	• *fought for women's rights* • *fought for civil rights*

Official USCIS Civics lesson

Susan B. Anthony was born in Massachusetts on February 15, 1820. She is known for campaigning for the right of women to vote. She spoke out publicly against slavery and for equal treatment of women in the workplace. In 1920, the 19th Amendment to the Constitution gave women the right to vote. Susan B. Anthony died 14 years before the adoption of the 19th Amendment, but it was still widely known as the Susan B. Anthony Amendment. In 1979, she became the first woman whose image appeared on a circulating U.S. coin. The coin is called the Susan B. Anthony dollar and is worth one dollar.

***Easy* Lesson**

Susan B. Anthony was born in Massachusetts on February 15, 1820. She is known for campaigning for the right of women to vote. In 1979, she became the first woman whose image appeared on a U.S. coin. The coin is called the Susan B. Anthony dollar.

Easy Answer!

Susan B. Anthony fought for civil rights.

Susan B. Anthony (8)

Q. 78	A. 78
Name <u>one</u> war fought by the United States in the 1900s.*	• *World War I* • *World War II* • *Korean War* • *Vietnam War* • *(Persian) Gulf War*

Official USCIS Civics lesson

The United States fought five wars in the 1900s: World War I, World War II, the Korean War, the Vietnam War, and the (Persian) Gulf War.

World War I began in 1914. It was a long and bloody struggle. The United States entered the war in 1917 after German submarines attacked British and U.S. ships, and the Germans contacted Mexico about starting a war against the United States. The war ended in 1918 when the Allied Powers (led by Britain, France, and the United States) defeated the Central Powers (led by Germany, Austria-Hungary, and the Ottoman Empire). The Treaty of Versailles officially ended the war in 1919. World War I was called "the war to end all wars." World War II began in 1939 when Germany invaded Poland. France and Great Britain then declared war on Germany. Germany had alliances with Italy and Japan, and together they formed the Axis powers.

The United States entered World War II in 1941, after the Japanese attacked Pearl Harbor, Hawaii. The United States joined France and Great Britain as the Allied powers and led the 1944 invasion of France known as D-Day. The liberation of Europe from German power was completed by May 1945. World War II did not end until Japan surrendered in August 1945.

The Korean War began in 1950 when the North Korean Army moved across the 38th parallel into South Korea. The 38th parallel was a boundary established after World War II. This boundary separated the northern area of Korea, which was under communist influence, from the southern area of Korea, which was allied with the United States. At the time, the United States was providing support to establish a democratic South Korean government. The United States provided military support to stop the advance of the North Korean Army. In the Korean conflict, democratic governments directly confronted communist governments.

The fighting ended in 1953, with the establishment of the countries of North Korea and South Korea.

From 1959 to 1975, United States Armed Forces and the South Vietnamese Army fought against the North Vietnamese in the Vietnam War. The United States supported the democratic government in the south of the country to help it resist pressure from the communist north. The war ended in 1975 with the temporary separation of the country into communist North Vietnam and democratic South Vietnam. In 1976, Vietnam was under total communist control. Almost 60,000 American men and women in the military died or were missing as a result of the Vietnam War.

On August 2, 1990, the Persian Gulf War began when Iraq invaded Kuwait. This invasion put the Iraqi Army closer to Saudi Arabia and its oil reserves, which supplied much of the world with oil. The United States and many other countries wanted to drive the Iraqi Army out of Kuwait and prevent it from invading other nearby countries. In January 1991, the United States led an international coalition of forces authorized by the United Nations into battle against the Iraqi Army. Within a month, the coalition had driven the Iraqis from Kuwait. The coalition declared a cease-fire on February 28, 1991.

Easy Lesson

The United States fought five wars in the 1900s: World War I, World War II, the Korean War, the Vietnam War, and the (Persian) Gulf War.

Easy Answer!

One war fought by the United States in the 1900s is World War II.

Q. 79	A. 79
Who was President during World War I?	• *(Woodrow) Wilson*

Official USCIS Civics lesson

Woodrow Wilson was the 28th president of the United States. President Wilson served two terms from 1913 to 1921. During his first term, he was able to keep the United States out of World War I. By 1917, Wilson knew this was no longer possible, and he asked Congress to declare war on Germany. On January 8,1918, he made a speech to Congress outlining "Fourteen Points" that justified the war and called for a plan to maintain peace after the war. President Wilson said, "We entered this war because violations of right had occurred which touched us to the quick and made the life of our own people impossible unless they were corrected and the world secure once for all against their recurrence." The war ended that year and Wilson traveled to Paris to work out the details of the surrender by Germany.

Easy **Lesson**

Woodrow Wilson was the 28th president of the United States. President Wilson served two terms from 1913 to 1921.

Easy Answer!

The President during World War I was Woodrow Wilson.

Q. 80	A. 80
Who was President during the Great Depression and World War II?	*(Franklin) Roosevelt*

Official USCIS Civics lesson

Franklin Delano Roosevelt (FDR) was president of the United States from 1933 until 1945. He was elected during the Great Depression, which was a period of economic crisis after the stock market crash of 1929. His program for handling the crisis was called "the New Deal." It included programs to create jobs and provided benefits and financial security for workers across the country. Under his leadership, the Social Security Administration (SSA) was established in 1935. Roosevelt led the nation into World War II after Japan's attack on Pearl Harbor in December 1941. He gave the country a sense of hope and strength during a time of great struggle. Roosevelt was elected to office four times. He died in 1945, early in his fourth term as president. His wife, Eleanor Roosevelt, was a human rights leader throughout her lifetime.

Easy Lesson

Franklin Delano Roosevelt (FDR) was president of the United States from 1933 until 1945. Roosevelt led the nation into World War II after Japan's attack on Pearl Harbor in December 1941.

Easy Answer!

The President during the Great Depression and Word War II was Franklin Roosevelt.

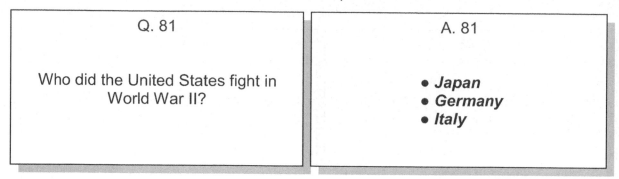

Q. 81	A. 81
Who did the United States fight in World War II?	• *Japan* • *Germany* • *Italy*

Official USCIS Civics lesson

The Japanese bombed U.S. naval bases in a surprise attack on Pearl Harbor, Hawaii, on December 7, 1941. The next day, President Franklin D. Roosevelt, as commander in chief of the military, obtained an official declaration of war from Congress. Japan's partners in the Axis, Italy and Germany, then declared war on the United States. The Allies fought against the German Nazis, the Italian Fascists, and Japan's military empire. This was truly a world war, with battles fought in Europe, Africa, Asia, and the Pacific Ocean.

***Easy* Lesson**

The Japanese bombed U.S. naval bases in a surprise attack on Pearl Harbor, Hawaii, on December 7, 1941. The next day, President Franklin D. Roosevelt obtained an official declaration of war from Congress. Japan's partners in the Axis, Italy and Germany. The Allies fought against the German Nazis, the Italian Fascists, and Japan's military empire.

Easy Answer!

In World War II, the United States fought Japan, Germany, and Italy.

Q. 82	A. 82
Before he was President, Eisenhower was a general. What war was he in?	• *World War II*

Official USCIS Civics lesson

Before becoming the 34th president of the United States in 1953, Dwight D. Eisenhower served as a major general in World War II. As commander of U.S. forces and supreme commander of the Allies in Europe, he led the successful D-Day invasion of Normandy, France, on June 6, 1944. In 1952, he retired from active service in the military. He was elected president of the United States later that year. As president, he established the interstate highway system and in 1953, the Department of Health, Education, and Welfare (now known as Health and Human Services) was created. He oversaw the end of the Korean War. Eisenhower left the White House in 1961, after serving two terms as president.

Easy **Lesson**

Before becoming the 34th president of the United States in 1953, Dwight D. Eisenhower served as a major general in World War II. Eisenhower left the White House in 1961, after serving two terms as president.

Easy Answer!

President Eisenhour was a general in World War II.

Dwight D. Eisenhour (12)

Q. 83	A. 83
During the Cold War, what was the main concern of the United States?	• *Communism*

Official USCIS Civics lesson

The main concern of the United States during the Cold War was the spread of communism. The Soviet Union (Union of Soviet Socialist Republics, or USSR) was a powerful nation that operated under the principles of communism. The United States and its allies believed that a democratic government and a capitalist economy were the best ways to preserve individual rights and freedoms. The United States and its allies feared the expansion of communism to countries outside the Soviet Union. The Cold War began shortly after the end of World War II and lasted for more than 40 years. It ended with the fall of the Berlin Wall in 1989, the reunification of East and West Germany in 1990, and the breakup of the USSR in 1991.

Easy Lesson

The main concern of the United States during the Cold War was the spread of communism. The Cold War began shortly after the end of World War II and lasted for more than 40 years. It ended with the fall of the Berlin Wall in 1989, the reunification of East and West Germany in 1990, and the breakup of the USSR in 1991.

Easy Answer!

During the Cold War, the main concern of the United States was Communism.

Q. 84	A. 84
What movement tried to end racial discrimination?	• *civil rights (movement)*

Official USCIS Civics lesson

The modern civil rights movement in the United States began in 1954 when the Supreme Court ruled that racial segregation in public schools was unconstitutional. The goal of the civil rights movement was to end racial discrimination against African Americans and to gain full and equal rights for Americans of all races. Using nonviolent strategies such as bus boycotts, sit-ins, and marches, people came together to demand social change. As a result, Congress passed the Civil Rights Act of 1964 and the Voting Rights Act of 1965. The Civil Rights Act made segregation in public facilities and racial discrimination in employment and education illegal. The law protects African Americans, women, and others from discrimination. The Voting Rights Act banned literacy tests and other special requirements that had been used to stop African Americans from registering to vote.

Easy Lesson

The goal of the civil rights movement was to end racial discrimination against African Americans and to gain full and equal rights for Americans of all races.

Easy Answer!

The movement that tried to end racial discrimination was the civil rights movement.

Q. 85	A. 85
What did Martin Luther King, Jr. do?*	• *fought for civil rights* • *worked for equality for all Americans*

Official USCIS Civics lesson

Martin Luther King, Jr. was a Baptist minister and civil rights leader. He worked hard to make America a more fair, tolerant, and equal nation. He was the main leader of the civil rights movement of the 1950s and 1960s. Because of this movement, civil rights laws were passed to protect voting rights and end racial segregation. King believed in the ideals of the Declaration of Independence—that every citizen deserves America's promise of equality and justice. In 1963, King delivered his famous "I Have a Dream" speech, which imagines an America in which people of all races exist together equally. He was only 35 years old when he received the Nobel Peace Prize in 1964 for his civil rights work. King was killed on April 4, 1968.

Easy Lesson

Martin Luther King, Jr. was a Baptist minister and civil rights leader. He worked hard to make America a more fair, tolerant, and equal nation. He was the main leader of the civil rights movement of the 1950s and 1960s. He was only 35 years old when he received the Nobel Peace Prize in 1964 for his civil rights work.

Easy Answer!

Martin Luther King, Jr. fought for civil rights.

Dr. Martin Luther King, Jr. (6)

Q. 86	A. 86
What major event happened on September 11, 2001, in the United States?	• **Terrorists attacked the United States**.

Official USCIS Civics lesson

On September 11, 2001, four airplanes flying out of U.S. airports were taken over by terrorists from the Al-Qaeda network of Islamic extremists. Two of the planes crashed into the World Trade Center's Twin Towers in New York City, destroying both buildings. One of the planes crashed into the Pentagon in Arlington, Virginia. The fourth plane, originally aimed at Washington, D.C., crashed in a field in Pennsylvania. Almost 3,000 people died in these attacks, most of them civilians. This was the worst attack on American soil in the history of the nation.

***Easy* Lesson**

On September 11, 2001, four airplanes flying out of U.S. airports were taken over by terrorists from the Al-Qaeda network of Islamic extremists. Two of the planes crashed into the World Trade Center's Twin Towers in New York City. One of the planes crashed into the Pentagon in Arlington, Virginia. The fourth plane, originally aimed at Washington, D.C., crashed in a field in Pennsylvania.

Easy Answer!

On September 11, 2001, terrorists attacked the United States.

Q. 87	A. 87
Name <u>one</u> American Indian tribe in the United States.	*Cherokee, Navajo, Sioux, Chippewa, Choctaw, Pueblo, Apache, Iroquois, Creek, Blackfeet, Seminole, Cheyenne, Arawak, Shawnee, Mohegan, Huron, Oneida, Lakota, Crow, Teton, Hopi, Inuit*

Official USCIS Civics lesson

American Indians lived in North America for thousands of years before the European settlers arrived. Today there are more than 500 federally recognized tribes in the United States. Each tribe has its own social and political system. American Indian cultures are different from one tribe to another, with different languages, beliefs, stories, music, and foods. Earlier in their history, some tribes settled in villages and farmed the land for food. Other tribes moved frequently as they hunted and gathered food and resources. The federal government signed treaties with American Indian tribes to move the tribes to reservations. These reservations are recognized as domestic, dependent nations.

***Easy* Lesson**

American Indians lived in North America for thousands of years before the European settlers arrived. Today there are more than 500 federally recognized tribes in the United States. The federal government signed treaties with American Indian tribes to move the tribes to reservations. These reservations are recognized as domestic, dependent nations.

Easy Answer!

One American Indian tribe in the United States is the Hopi tribe.

Q. 88	A. 88
Name <u>one</u> of the two longest rivers in the United States.	• *Missouri (River)* • *Mississippi (River)*

Official USCIS Civics lesson

The Mississippi River is one of America's longest rivers. It runs through 10 U.S. states. The Mississippi River was used by American Indians for trade, food, and water before Europeans came to America. It is nicknamed the "Father of Waters." Today, the Mississippi River is a major shipping route and a source of drinking water for millions of people. The Missouri River is also one of the longest rivers in the United States. The Missouri River is actually longer than the Mississippi River. It starts in Montana and flows into the Mississippi River. In 1673, the French explorers Jolliet and Marquette were the first Europeans to find the Missouri River. It is nicknamed "Big Muddy" because of its high silt content.

***Easy* Lesson**

The Mississippi River is one of America's longest rivers. It runs through 10 U.S. states. The Mississippi River was used by American Indians for trade, food, and water before Europeans came to America.

Easy Answer!

One of the two longest rivers in the United States is the Mississippi River.

Q. 89	A. 89
What ocean is on the West Coast of the United States?	• *Pacific (Ocean)*

Official USCIS Civics lesson

The Pacific Ocean is on the West Coast of the United States. It is the largest ocean on Earth and covers one-third of the Earth's surface. The Pacific Ocean is important to the U.S. economy because of its many natural resources such as fish. Europeans first learned about the Pacific Ocean in the 16th century. Spanish explorer Vasco Núñez de Balboa reached the ocean in 1514 when he crossed the Isthmus of Panama. Later, Ferdinand Magellan sailed across the Pacific as he traveled around the Earth in search of spices. "Pacific" means "peaceful." Magellan named the Pacific Ocean the "peaceful sea," because there were no storms on his trip from Spain to the spice world. The U.S. states that border the Pacific Ocean are Alaska, Washington, Oregon, California, and Hawaii.

Easy Lesson

The Pacific Ocean is on the West Coast of the United States. It is the largest ocean on Earth and covers one-third of the Earth's surface.

Easy Answer!

The ocean that is on the West Coast of the United States is the Pacific Ocean.

Q. 90	A. 90
What ocean is on the East Coast of the United States?	● *Atlantic (Ocean)*

Official USCIS Civics lesson

The Atlantic Ocean is on the East Coast of the United States. The ocean was named after the giant Atlas from Greek mythology. It is the second largest ocean in the world. The Atlantic Ocean is a major sea route for ships. It is one of the most frequently traveled oceans in the world. The Atlantic Ocean is also a source of many natural resources. The Atlantic Ocean was formed by the separation of the North American and European continents millions of years ago. The ocean covers about one-fifth of the Earth's surface. In the middle of the ocean is the Mid-Atlantic Ridge, an immense underwater mountain range that extends the length of the Atlantic and is a source of volcanic activity. The U.S. states that border the Atlantic Ocean are Connecticut, Delaware, Florida, Georgia, Maine, Maryland, Massachusetts, New Hampshire, New Jersey, New York, North Carolina, Rhode Island, South Carolina, and Virginia.

Easy **Lesson**

The Atlantic Ocean is on the East Coast of the United States. It is the second largest ocean in the world.

Easy Answer!

The ocean that is on the East Coast of the United States is the Atlantic Ocean.

Q. 91	A. 91
Name <u>one</u> U.S. territory.	• **_Puerto Rico_** • **_U.S. Virgin Islands_** • **_American Samoa_** • **_Northern Mariana Islands_** • **_Guam_**

Official USCIS Civics lesson

There are five major U.S. territories: American Samoa, Guam, the Northern Mariana Islands, Puerto Rico, and the U.S. Virgin Islands. A U.S. territory is a partially self-governing piece of land under the authority of the U.S. government. U.S. territories are not states, but they do have representation in Congress. Each territory is allowed to send a delegate to the House of Representatives. The people who live in American Samoa are considered U.S. nationals; the people in the other four territories are U.S. citizens. Citizens of the territories can vote in primary elections for president, but they cannot vote in the general elections for president.

Easy Lesson

A U.S. territory is a partially self-governing piece of land under the authority of the U.S. government. U.S. territories are not states, but they do have representation in Congress. Each territory is allowed to send a delegate to the House of Representatives.

Easy Answer!

One U.S. territory is Puerto Rico.

Q. 92	A. 92
Name <u>one</u> state that borders Canada.	• **Maine** • **New Hampshire** • **Vermont** • **New York** • **Pennsylvania** • **Ohio** • **Michigan** • **Minnesota** • **North Dakota** • **Montana** • **Idaho** • **Washington** • **Alaska**

Official USCIS Civics lesson

The northern border of the United States stretches more than 5,000 miles from Maine in the East to Alaska in the West. There are 13 states on the border with Canada. The Treaty of Paris of 1783 established the official boundary between Canada and the United States after the Revolutionary War. Since that time, there have been land disputes, but they have been resolved through treaties. The International Boundary Commission, which is headed by two commissioners, one American and one Canadian, is responsible for maintaining the boundary.

***Easy* Lesson**

The northern border of the United States stretches more than 5,000 miles from Maine in the East to Alaska in the West. There are 13 states on the border with Canada

Easy Answer!

One state that borders Canada is New York.

Q. 93	A. 93
Name <u>one</u> state that borders Mexico.	• *California* • *Arizona* • *New Mexico* • *Texas*

Official USCIS Civics lesson

The border between the United States and Mexico is about 1,900 miles long and spans four U.S. states—Arizona, California, New Mexico, and Texas. The United States established the border with Mexico after the Mexican-American War and the Gadsden Purchase in 1853. The Gadsden Purchase helped the United States get the land it needed to expand the southern railroad. The United States bought this land for $10 million. The land bought through the Gadsden Purchase is now part of the states of Arizona and New Mexico. The U.S. border with Mexico is one of the busiest international borders in the world.

Easy **Lesson**

The border between the United States and Mexico is about 1,900 miles long and spans four U.S. states—Arizona, California, New Mexico, and Texas.

Easy Answer!

One state that borders Mexico is New Mexico.

Q. 94	A. 94
What is the capital of the United States?*	• *Washington, D.C.*

Official USCIS Civics lesson

When the Constitution established our nation in 1789, the capital of the United States was in New York City. Congress soon began discussing the location of a permanent capital city. In Congress, representatives of northern states argued with representatives of southern states. Each side wanted the capital to be in its own region. As part of the Compromise of 1790, the capital would be located in the South. In return, the North did not have to pay the debt it owed from the Revolutionary War. George Washington chose a location for the capital along the Potomac River between Maryland and Virginia. As part of the compromise, Philadelphia, Pennsylvania, became the temporary new location for the capital. In 1800, after 10 years, the capital was moved to its current location of Washington, D.C.

Easy **Lesson**

George Washington chose a location for the capital along the Potomac River between Maryland and Virginia. The capital is now known as Washington, D.C. (D.C. is the abbreviation for "District of Columbia".)

Easy Answer!

The capital of the United States is Washington D.C.

Q. 95	A. 95
Where is the Statue of Liberty?*	• **New York (Harbor)** • **Liberty Island** • **New Jersey** • **near New York City** • **on the Hudson (River)**

Official USCIS Civics lesson

The Statue of Liberty is on Liberty Island, a 12-acre island in the New York harbor. France gave the statue to the United States as a gift of friendship. French artist Frederic-Auguste Bartholdi made the statue. It shows a woman escaping the chains of tyranny and holding a torch symbolizing liberty. The Statue of Liberty was dedicated on October 28, 1886, 110 years after the signing of the Declaration of Independence. President Grover Cleveland accepted the gift for the American people. The Statue of Liberty is a well-known symbol of the United States and of freedom and democracy. The Statue of Liberty became a symbol of immigration because it was located next to Ellis Island, which was the first entry point for many immigrants during the great waves of immigration. The Statue of Liberty was the first thing new immigrants saw as they approached New York harbor.

***Easy* Lesson**

The Statue of Liberty is on Liberty Island, a 12-acre island in the New York harbor.

Easy Answer!

The Statue of Liberty is near New York City.

Statue of Liberty (6)

Q. 96	A. 96
Why does the flag have 13 stripes?	• **because there were 13 original colonies** • **because the stripes represent the original colonies**

Official USCIS Civics lesson

There are 13 stripes on the flag because there were 13 original colonies. We call the American flag "the Stars and Stripes." For 18 years after the United States became an independent country, the flag had only 13 stripes. In 1794, Kentucky and Vermont joined the United States, and two stripes were added to the flag. In 1818, Congress decided that the number of stripes on the flag should always be 13. This would honor the original states that were colonies of Great Britain before America's independence.

***Easy* Lesson**

There are 13 stripes on the flag because there were 13 original colonies. We call the American flag "the Stars and Stripes." In 1818, Congress decided that the number of stripes on the flag should always be 13.

Easy Answer!

The flag has 13 stripes because there were 13 original colonies.

Q. 97	A. 97
Why does the flag have 50 stars?*	• *because there is one star for each state* • *because each star represents a state* • *because there are 50 states*

Official USCIS Civics lesson

Each star on the flag represents a state. This is why the number of stars has changed over the years from 13 to 50. The number of stars reached 50 in 1959, when Hawaii joined the United States as the 50th state. In 1777, the Second Continental Congress passed the first Flag Act, stating, "Resolved, That the flag of the United States be made of thirteen stripes, alternate red and white; that the union be thirteen stars, white in a blue field, representing a new Constellation."

Easy Lesson

Each star on the flag represents a state. This is why the number of stars has changed over the years from 13 to 50.

Easy Answer!

The flag has 50 stars because there are 50 states.

American Flag (6)

Q. 98	A. 98
What is the name of the national anthem?	• *The Star-Spangled Banner*

Official USCIS Civics lesson

During the War of 1812, British soldiers invaded the United States. On the night of September 13, 1814, British warships bombed Fort McHenry. This fort protected the city of Baltimore, Maryland. An American named Francis Scott Key watched the bombing and thought that the fort would fall. As the sun rose the next morning, Key looked toward the fort. He saw that the flag above the fort was still flying. This let him know that the British had not defeated the Americans. Key immediately wrote the words to a poem he called the "Defence of Fort M'Henry." The words of the poem became "The Star-Spangled Banner." Congress passed a law in 1931 naming "The Star-Spangled Banner" the official national anthem. Here are the words to the first verse of the national anthem: The Star-Spangled Banner Oh, say, can you see, by the dawn's early light, What so proudly we hailed at the twilight's last gleaming? Whose broad stripes and bright stars, thro' the perilous fight; O'er the ramparts we watched, were so gallantly streaming. And the rockets' red glare, the bombs bursting in air, Gave proof through the night that our flag was still there. Oh, say, does that star-spangled banner yet wave O'er the land of the free and the home of the brave?

Easy Lesson

During the War of 1812, Francis Scott Key watched the bombing of a fort and thought that the fort would fall. As the sun rose the next morning, Key looked toward the fort. He saw that the flag above the fort was still flying. Key immediately wrote the words to a poem which later became "The Star-Spangled Banner."

Easy Answer!

The name of the national anthem is The Star-Spangled Banner.

Q. 99	A. 99
When do we celebrate Independence Day?*	• *July 4*

Official USCIS Civics lesson

In the United States, we celebrate Independence Day on July 4 to mark the anniversary of the adoption of the Declaration of Independence. After signing the Declaration of Independence, John Adams wrote to his wife, "I am apt to believe that it will be celebrated, by succeeding Generations, as the great anniversary Festival." The Declaration of Independence, written by Thomas Jefferson, explained why the colonies had decided to separate from Great Britain. Americans celebrate the Fourth of July as the birthday of America, with parades, fireworks, patriotic songs, and readings of the Declaration of Independence.

***Easy* Lesson**

In the United States, we celebrate Independence Day on July 4 to mark the anniversary of the adoption of the Declaration of Independence.

Easy Answer!

We celebrate Independence Day on July 4.

Q. 100	A. 100
Name <u>two</u> national U.S. holidays.	• *New Year's Day,* • *Martin Luther King, Jr. Day,* • *Presidents' Day,* • *Memorial Day,* • *Independence Day,* • *Labor Day,* • *Columbus Day,* • *Veterans Day,* • *Thanksgiving,* • *Christmas*

Official USCIS Civics lesson

Many Americans celebrate national or federal holidays. These holidays often honor people or events in our American heritage. These holidays are "national" in a legal sense only for federal institutions and in the District of Columbia. Typically, federal offices are closed on these holidays. Each state can decide whether or not to celebrate the holiday. Businesses, schools, and commercial establishments may choose whether or not to close on these days. Since 1971, federal holidays are observed on Mondays except for New Year's Day, Independence Day, Veterans Day, Thanksgiving, and Christmas.

Easy **Lesson**

These holidays are "national" in a legal sense only for federal institutions and in the District of Columbia. Typically, federal offices are closed on these holidays.

Easy Answer!

Two national U.S. holidays are Columbus Day and Thanksgiving.

Reading Words and Practice Exercises	6

The following are all the words you must know how to read.

People	Civics	Places	Holidays
Abraham Lincoln George Washington	American flag Bill of Rights capital citizen city Congress country Father of Our Country government President right senators state / states White House	America U.S. United States	Presidents' Day Memorial Day Flag Day Independence Day Labor Day Columbus Day Thanksgiving

Question Words	Verbs	Other	
How What When Where Who Why	can come do/does elects have / has is / are / was / be lives / lived meet name pay vote want	a for here in of on the to we	colors dollar bill first largest many most north one people second south

Reading Sentences

The following are 100 sentences for you to practice reading the words. They contain all the words that you must know how to read. Have a friend or relative read a sentence, and then you read the sentence. Have the friend or relative tell you if you are reading the sentence correctly. Remember, the more you practice, the better you will do.

1. Pay here.

2. We want to pay.

3. We want to vote.

4. What is Flag Day?

5. Why be the first?

6. When is Labor Day?

7. Be first to vote.

8. Where is the south?

9. Where do we pay?

10. The senators are here.

11. When do people vote?

12. Where is the north?

13. Who elects Congress?

14. When is Memorial Day?

15. When does one vote?

16. What is Thanksgiving?

17. What is the Congress?

18. We lived in the south.

19. When does Flag Day come?

20. Who can be a citizen?

21. Why do people vote?

22. America is in the north.

23. The capital is a city.

24. When is Independence Day?

25. America is a country.

26. When is Presidents' Day?

27. Where is the largest city?

28. The President was here.

29. When do the people vote?

30. We can meet the President.

31. Most senators are here.

32. We can meet the Senators.

33. We want to do what is right.

34. The largest city is here.

35. Who was Abraham Lincoln?

36. The White House is here.

37. Come here on Labor Day.

38. Where is the dollar bill?

39. Who elects the U.S. senators?

40. How does a citizen vote?

41. Where is the White House?

42. When is Independence Day?

43. The capital is in the north.

44. Name a state in the south.

45. Abraham Lincoln lived here.

46. The south has many people.

47. People lived in many states.

48. Who was George Washington?

49. Who is the first citizen?

50. A citizen has to vote here.

51. Was Abraham Lincoln a President?

52. Where do we meet the senators?

53. What is the Bill of Rights?

54. Name one right of a citizen.

55. Who lives in the White House?

56. People come in many colors.

57. What is the largest state?

58. Why do people want to vote?

59. Most states are in the north.

60. What is the largest country?

61. Senators meet in the capital.

62. The north has the most people.

63. The American flag has colors.

64. Who was the second President?

65. The people elect the Congress.

66. Abraham Lincoln was a President.

67. George Washington lived here.

68. Many states are in the south.

69. The United States is a country.

70. What is the Bill of Rights?

71. Many people lived in the south.

72. The government has many senators.

73. What country is south of the U.S.?

74. Who is the Father of Our Country?

75. Senators meet in the capital city.

76. The largest state is in the north.

77. The second name is Abraham Lincoln.

78. The government is for the people.

79. How many rights do citizens have?

80. What country is north of the U.S.?

81. How many Senators are in Congress?

82. What is the name of the President?

83. Abraham Lincoln lived in the north.

84. Where is the capital of the country?

85. The President is the first citizen.

86. When are Columbus Day and Thanksgiving?

87. United States people have many rights.

88. The President lives in the White House.

89. George Washington is on the dollar bill.

90. George Washington was the first President.

91. Presidents' Day and Memorial Day come first.

92. The second President lived in the south.

93. The capital of the United States is a city.

94. How many colors does the American flag have?

95. Citizens vote for the government of America.

96. Why is George Washington on the dollar bill?

97. Abraham Lincoln was a United States President.

98. What is the name of the Father of Our Country?

99. The father of our country is George Washington.

100. Where is the largest city in the United States?

Writing Words and Practice Sentences	7

The following are all the words you must know how to write.

People	Civics	Places	Months
Adams Lincoln Washington	American Indians capital citizens Civil War Congress Father of Our Country flag free freedom of speech President Right Senators State / states White House	Alaska California Canada Delaware Mexico New York City United States Washington Washington, D.C.	February May June July September October November

Verbs	Holidays	Other	
can come elect have/has is / was / be lives / lived meets pay vote want	Presidents' Day Memorial Day Flag Day Independence Day Labor Day Columbus Day Thanksgiving	and during for here in of on the to we	blue dollar bill fifty / 50 first largest most north one one hundred /100 people red second south taxes white

Writing Words

The following sentences contain all the words that you need to know how to write. Have a friend or relative read each sentence to you, and then write the sentence. Check to see if you spelled each word correctly. As with everything else, the more you practice, the better you will do.

1. We pay taxes.

2. The flag is here.

3. Citizens can vote.

4. People can be free.

5. Alaska is a state.

6. Pay for the flag.

7. We want to vote.

8. Citizens pay taxes.

9. We lived in Canada.

10. Pay here for the flag.

11. Most people can vote.

12. Flag Day is in June.

13. Pay for the largest flag.

14. The largest flag is free.

15. Senators vote for taxes.

16. One state is Delaware.

17. People want to be free.

18. Adams was President

19. Washington is one State.

20. The Senators vote here.

21. Citizens elect the Senators.

22. Alaska is the largest state.

23. Alaska is north of Mexico.

24. Mexico is south of Canada.

25. Memorial Day is in May.

26. Independence Day is in July.

27. Labor Day is in September.

28. Columbus Day is in October.

29. The Senators want to vote.

30. The White House is white.

31. Delaware is north of Mexico.

32. Citizens vote in November.

33. Come to the White House.

34. Is Canada the largest state?

35. American Indians can vote.

36. One Right is the right to vote.

37. The largest state is Alaska.

38. Thanksgiving is in November.

39. Citizens elect the President.

40. We the citizens elect Congress.

41. The White House is here.

42. American Indians in Alaska vote.

43. The second President was Adams.

44. The right to vote is one right.

45. Citizens want freedom of speech.

46. The President meets the people.

47. The White House is in the capital.

48. United States citizens pay taxes.

49. Is Washington, D.C. in Washington?

50. Congress meets in Washington, D.C.

51. California has the most people.

52. Presidents day is in February.

53. Washington is on the dollar bill.

54. Unites States citizens can vote.

55. Lincoln lived in the White House.

56. The flag is red, white and blue.

57. American Indians lived in Alaska.

58. Freedom of speech is one Right.

59. California is south of Washington.

60. The President lives in Washington, D.C.

61. New York City has the most people.

62. Adams was the second President.

63. One Right is freedom of speech.

64. Freedom of speech is one Right.

65. Washington was the first President.

66. The first President was Washington.

67. The people lived in Washington.

68. People come during Thanksgiving.

69. We can come to the White House.

70. Canada is north of the United States.

71. Mexico is south of the United States.

72. Delaware is south of New York City.

73. New York City is in the United States.

74. Come during Independence Day.

75. Most people have one dollar bill.

76. New York City is the largest one.

77. New York City is north of Delaware.

78. The White House is in Washington, D.C.

79. The United States has fifty (50) states.

80. The President lives in the White House.

81. Washington is the Father of Our Country.

82. People come here for freedom of speech.

83. Congress has one hundred (100) Senators.

84. The White House has the largest flag.

85. We have the Right of freedom of speech.

86. The Father of Our Country is Washington.

87. Lincoln was President during the Civil War.

88. Alaska is the largest of the 50 (fifty) states.

89. People come to the United States to be free.

90. People want American Indians to vote.

91. The President meets people at the White House.

92. Citizens elect the President and the Senators.

93. The President and the Senators pay taxes.

94. During the Civil War the President was Lincoln.

95. American Indians lived first in the United States.

96. The capital of the United States is Washington, D.C.

97. American Indians lived in the United States first.

98. One President lived in Washington D.C. and New York City.

99. Presidents' Day and Memorial Day come before Thanksgiving.

100. The one hundred (100) Senators vote in Washington, D.C.

House of Representative Members (Congressmen) (435)

8

The number before the name is the Congressional District that the person represents..

FEBRUARY 15, 2019

ALABAMA
1 Bradley Byrne
2 Martha Roby
3 Mike Rogers
4 Robert B. Aderholt
5 Mo Brooks
6 Gary J. Palmer
7 Terri A. Sewell

ALASKA
AT LARGE Don Young

ARIZONA
1 Tom O'Halleran
2 Ann Kirkpatrick
3 Raúl M. Grijalva
4 Paul A. Gosar
5 Andy Biggs
6 David Schweikert
7 Ruben Gallego
8 Debbie Lesko
9 Greg Stanton

ARKANSAS
1 Eric A. "Rick" Crawford
2 J. French Hill
3 Steve Womack
4 Bruce Westerman

CALIFORNIA
1 Doug LaMalfa
2 Jared Huffman
3 John Garamendi
4 Tom McClintock
5 Mike Thompson
6 Doris O. Matsui
7 Ami Bera
8 Paul Cook
9 Jerry McNerney
10 Josh Harder

11 Mark DeSaulnier
12 Nancy Pelosi
13 Barbara Lee
14 Jackie Speier
15 Eric Swalwell
16 Jim Costa
17 Ro Khanna
18 Anna G. Eshoo
19 Zoe Lofgren
20 Jimmy Panetta
21 TJ Cox
22 Devin Nunes
23 Kevin McCarthy
24 Salud O. Carbajal
25 Vacant
26 Julia Brownley
27 Judy Chu
28 Adam Schiff
29 Tony Cárdenas
30 Brad Sherman
31 Pete Aguilar
32 Grace F. Napolitano
33 Ted Lieu
34 Jimmy Gomez
35 Norma J. Torres
36 Raul Ruiz
37 Karen Bass
38 Linda T. Sánchez
39 Gilbert Ray Cisneros, Jr.
40 Lucille Roybal-Allard
41 Mark Takano
42 Ken Calvert
43 Maxine Waters
44 Nanette Diaz Barragán
45 Katie Porter
46 J. Luis Correa
47 Alan S. Lowenthal
48 Harley Rouda
49 Mike Levin
50 Vacant
51 Juan Vargas
52 Scott H. Peters

53 Susan A. Davis

COLORADO
1 Diana DeGette
2 Joe Neguse
3 Scott R. Tipton
4 Ken Buck
5 Doug Lamborn
6 Jason Crow
7 Ed Perlmutter

CONNECTICUT
1 John B. Larson
2 Joe Courtney
3 Rosa L. DeLauro
4 James A. Himes
5 Jahana Hayes

DELAWARE
AT LARGE
Lisa Blunt Rochester

FLORIDA
1 Matt Gaetz
2 Neal P. Dunn
3 Ted S. Yoho
4 John H. Rutherford
5 Al Lawson, Jr.
6 Michael Waltz
7 Stephanie N. Murphy
8 Bill Posey
9 Darren Soto
10 Val Butler Demings
11 Daniel Webster
12 Gus M. Bilirakis
13 Charlie Crist
14 Kathy Castor
15 Ross Spano
16 Vern Buchanan
17 W. Gregory Steube
18 Brian J. Mast
19 Francis Rooney

20 Alcee L. Hastings
21 Lois Frankel
22 Theodore E. Deutch
23 Debbie Wasserman
  Schultz
24 Frederica S. Wilson
25 Mario Diaz-Balart
26 Debbie Mucarsel-Powell
27 Donna E. Shalala

GEORGIA
1 Earl L. "Buddy" Carter
2 Sanford D. Bishop, Jr.
3 A. Drew Ferguson IV
4 Henry "Hank" Johnson, Jr.
5 John Lewis .
6 Lucy McBath
7 Rob Woodall .
8 Austin Scott
9 Doug Collins
10 Jody B. Hice
11 Barry Loudermilk
12 Rick W. Allen
13 David Scott
14 Tom Graves

HAWAII
1 Ed Case
2 Tulsi Gabbard

IDAHO
1 Russ Fulcher
2 Michael K. Simpson

ILLINOIS
1 Bobby L. Rush
2 Robin L. Kelly
3 Daniel Lipinski
4 Jesús G. "Chuy" García
5 Mike Quigley
6 Sean Casten
7 Danny K. Davis
8 Raja Krishnamoorthi
9 Janice D. Schakowsky
10 Bradley Scott Schneider
11 Bill Foster
12 Mike Bost
13 Rodney Davis
14 Lauren Underwood
15 John Shimkus
16 Adam Kinzinger

17 Cheri Bustos
18 Darin LaHood

INDIANA
1 Peter J. Visclosky
2 Jackie Walorski
3 Jim Banks
4 James R. Baird
5 Susan W. Brooks
6 Greg Pence
7 André Carson
8 Larry Bucshon
9 Trey Hollingsworth

IOWA
1 Abby Finkenauer
2 David Loebsack
3 Cynthia Axne
4 Steve King

KANSAS
1 Roger W. Marshall
2 Steve Watkins
3 Sharice Davids
4 Ron Estes

KENTUCKY
1 James Comer
2 Brett Guthrie
3 John A. Yarmuth
4 Thomas Massie
5 Harold Rogers
6 Andy Barr

LOUISIANA
1 Steve Scalise
2 Cedric L. Richmond
3 Clay Higgins
4 Mike Johnson
5 Ralph Lee Abraham
6 Garret Graves

MAINE
1 Chellie Pingree
2 Jared F. Golden

MARYLAND
1 Andy Harris
2 C. A. Dutch Ruppersberger
3 John P. Sarbanes
4 Anthony G. Brown

5 Steny H. Hoyer
6 David J. Trone
7 Vacancy
8 Jamie Raskin

MASSACHUSETTS
1 Richard E. Neal
2 James P. McGovern
3 Lori Trahan
4 Joseph P. Kennedy III
5 Katherine M. Clark
6 Seth Moulton
7 Ayanna Pressley
8 Stephen F. Lynch
9 William R. Keating

MICHIGAN
1 Jack Bergman
2 Bill Huizenga
3 Justin Amash
4 John R. Moolenaar
5 Daniel T. Kildee
6 Fred Upton
7 Tim Walbergn
8 Elissa Slotkin
9 Andy Levin
10 Paul Mitchell
11 Haley M. Stevens
12 Debbie Dingell
13 Rashida Tlaib
14 Brenda L. Lawrence

MINNESOTA
1 Jim Hagedorn
2 Angie Craig
3 Dean Phillips
4 Betty McCollum
5 Ilhan Omar
6 Tom Emmer
7 Collin C. Peterson
8 Pete Stauber

MISSISSIPPI
1 Trent Kelly
2 Bennie G. Thompson
3 Michael Guest
4 Steven M. Palazzo

MISSOURI
1 Lacy Clay, Jr.
2 Ann Wagner

3 Blaine Luetkemeyer
4 Vicky Hartzler
5 Emanuel Cleaver
6 Sam Graves
7 Billy Long
8 Jason Smith

MONTANA
AT LARGE
Greg Gianforte

NEBRASKA
1 Jeff Fortenberry
2 Don Bacon
3 Adrian Smith

NEVADA
1 Dina Titus
2 Mark E. Amodei
3 Susie Lee
4 Steven Horsford

NEW HAMPSHIRE
1 Chris Pappas
2 Ann M. Kuster

NEW JERSEY
1 Donald Norcross
2 Jefferson Van Drew
3 Andy Kim
4 Christopher H. Smith
5 Josh Gottheimer
6 Frank Pallone, Jr.
7 Tom Malinowski .
8 Albio Sires
9 Bill Pascrell, Jr.
10 Donald M. Payne, Jr.
11 Mikie Sherrill
12 Bonnie Watson Coleman

NEW MEXICO
1 Debra A. Haaland
2 Xochitl Torres Small
3 Ben Ray Luján

NEW YORK
1 Lee M. Zeldin
2 Peter T. King
3 Thomas R. Suozzi
4 Kathleen M. Rice
5 Gregory W. Meeks

6 Grace Meng
7 Nydia M. Velázquez
8 Hakeem S. Jeffries
9 Yvette D. Clarke ..
10 Jerrold Nadler
11 Max Rose
12 Carolyn B. Maloney
13 Adriano Espaillat
14 Alexandria Ocasio-Cortez
15 José E. Serrano
16 Eliot L. Engel
17 Nita Lowey
18 Sean Patrick Maloney
19 Antonio Delgado k
20 Paul Tonko
21 Elise M. Stefanik
22 Anthony Brindisi
23 Tom Reed
24 John Katko .
25 Joseph D. Morelle
26 Brian Higgins
27 Vacancy

NORTH CAROLINA
1 G. K. Butterfield
2 George Holding
3 Gregory Francis Murphy
4 David E. Price
5 Virginia Foxx
6 Mark Walker
7 David Rouzer
8 Richard Hudson
9 Dan Bishop
10 Patrick T. McHenry
11 Mark Meadows
12 Alma S. Adams
13 Ted Budd

NORTH DAKOTA
AT LARGE
Kelly Armstrong

OHIO
1 Steve Chabot
2 Brad R. Wenstrup
3 Joyce Beatty
4 Jim Jordan
5 Robert E. Latta
6 Bill Johnson
7 Bob Gibbs
8 Warren Davidson

9 Marcy Kaptur
10 Michael R. Turner
11 Marcia L. Fudge
12 Troy Balderson
13 Tim Ryan
14 David P. Joyce
15 Steve Stivers
16 Anthony Gonzalez

OKLAHOMA
1 Kevin Hern
2 Markwayne Mullin
3 Frank D. Lucas
4 Tom Cole
5 Kendra S. Horn

OREGON
1 Suzanne Bonamici
2 Greg Walden
3 Earl Blumenauer
4 Peter A. DeFazio
5 Kurt Schrader

PENNSYLVANIA
1 Brian K. Fitzpatrick
2 Brendan F. Boyle
3 Dwight Evans
4 Madeleine Dean
5 Mary Gay Scanlone
6 Chrissy Houlahan
7 Susan Wild
8 Matt Cartwright
9 Daniel Meuser
10 Scott Perry
11 Lloyd Smucker
12 Fred Keller
13 John Joyce
14 Guy Reschenthaler
15 Glenn Thompson
16 Mike Kelly
17 Conor Lamb
18 Michael F. Doyle

RHODE ISLAND
1 David N. Cicilline
2 James R. Langevin

SOUTH CAROLINA
1 Joe Cunningham
2 Joe Wilson
3 Jeff Duncan

4 William R. Timmons IV
5 Ralph Norman
6 James E. Clyburn
7 Tom Rice

SOUTH DAKOTA
AT LARGE
Dusty Johnson

TENNESSEE
1 Phil Roe
2 Tim Burchett
3 Charles J. "Chuck" Fleischmann
4 Scott DesJarlais
5 Jim Cooper
6 John W. Rose
7 Mark E. Green
8 David Kustoff
9 Steve Cohen

TEXAS
1 Louie Gohmert
2 Dan Crenshaw
3 Van Taylor
4 John Ratcliffeh
5 Lance Gooden
6 Ron Wright
7 Lizzie Fletcher
8 Kevin Brady
9 Al Green
10 Michael T. McCaul
11 K. Michael Conaway
12 Kay Granger
13 Mac Thornberry
14 Randy K. Weber, Sr.
15 Vicente Gonzalez
16 Veronica Escobar
17 Bill Flores
18 Sheila Jackson Lee
19 Jodey C. Arrington
20 Joaquin Castro
21 Chip Roy
22 Pete Olson
23 Will Hurd
24 Kenny Marchant

25 Roger Williams
26 Michael C. Burgess
27 Michael Cloud
28 Henry Cuellar
29 Sylvia R. Garcia
30 Eddie Bernice Johnson
31 John R. Carter
32 Colin Z. Allred
33 Marc A. Veasey
34 Filemon Vela
35 Lloyd Doggett
36 Brian Babin

UTAH
1 Rob Bishop
2 Chris Stewart
3 John R. Curtis
4 Ben McAdams

VERMONT
AT LARGE
Peter Welch

VIRGINIA
1 Robert J. Wittman
2 Elaine G. Luria
3 Robert C. "Bobby" Scott
4 A. Donald McEachin
5 Denver Riggleman
6 Ben Cline
7 Abigail Davis Spanberger
8 Donald S. Beyer, Jr.
9 H. Morgan Griffith
10 Jennifer Wexton
11 Gerald E. Connolly

WASHINGTON
1 Suzan K. DelBene
2 Rick Larsen
3 Jaime Herrera Beutler
4 Dan Newhouse
5 Cathy McMorris Rodgers
6 Derek Kilmer
7 Pramila Jayapal
8 Kim Schrier
9 Adam Smith

10 Denny Heck

WEST VIRGINIA
1 David B. McKinley
2 Alexander X. Mooney
3 Carol D. Miller

WISCONSIN
1 Bryan Steil
2 Mark Pocan
3 Ron Kind
4 Gwen Moore
5 F. James Sensenbrenner, Jr.
6 Glenn Grothman
7 Vacancy
8 Mike Gallagher

WYOMING
AT LARGE
Liz Cheney

PUERTO RICO
RESIDENT COMMISSIONER
Jenniffer González-Colón

AMERICAN SAMOA
DELEGATE
Amata Coleman Radewagen

DISTRICT OF COLUMBIA
DELEGATE
Eleanor Holmes Norton

GUAM
DELEGATE
Michael F. Q. San Nicolas

NORTHERN MARIANA ISLANDS
DELEGATE
Gregorio Kilili Camacho Sablan

VIRGIN ISLANDS
DELEGATE
Stacey E. Plaskett

US Senators (50 States)			9
State	**Senators**	**State**	**Senators**
Alabama	1. Doug Jones 2. Richard C. Shelby	**Indiana**	1. Mike Braun 2. Todd Young
Alaska	1. Lisa Murkowski 2. Dan Sullivan	**Iowa**	1. Joni Ernst 2. Chuck Grassley
Arizona	1. Martha McSally 2. Kyrsten Sinema	**Kansas**	1. Jerry Moran 2. Pat Roberts
Arkansas	1. John Boozman 2. Tom Cotton	**Kentucky**	1. Mitch McConnell 2. Rand Paul
California	1. Dianne Feinstein 2. Kamala Harris	**Louisiana**	1. Bill Cassidy 2. John Kennedy
Colorado	1. Michael F. Bennett 2. Cory Gardner	**Maine**	1. Susan M. Collins 2. Angus S. King, Jr.
Connecticut	1. Richard Blumenthal 2. Christopher Murphy	**Maryland**	1. Benjamin Cardin 2. Chris Van Hollen
Delaware	1. Thomas R. Carper 2. Christopher A. Coons	**Massachusetts**	1. Edward J. Markey 2. Elizabeth D. Warren
Florida	1. Marco Rubio 2. Rick Scott	**Michigan**	1. Gary C. Peters 2. Debbie Stabenow
Georgia	1. Kelly Loeffler 2. David Perdue	**Minnesota**	1. Amy Klobuchar 2. Tina Smith
Hawaii	1. Mazie K. Hirono 2. Brian Schatz	**Mississippi**	1. Cindy Hyde-Smith 2. Roger F. Wicker
Idaho	1. Mike Crapo 2. James E. Risch	**Missouri**	1. Roy Blunt 2. Josh R. Hawley
Illinois	1. Tammy Duckworth 2. Richard J. Durbin	**Montana**	1. Steve Daines 2. Jon Tester

State	Senators	State	Senators
Nebraska	1. Deb Fischer 2. Ben Sasse	South Carolina	1. Lindsey Graham 2. Tim Scott
Nevada	1. Catherine Cortez Masto 2. Jacky Rosen	South Dakota	1. Mike Rounds 2. John Thune
New Hampshire	1. Margaret Wood Hassan 2. Jeanne Shaheen	Tennessee	1. Lamar Alexander 2. Marsha Blackburn
New Jersey	1. Cory Booker 2. Robert Menendez	Texas	1. John Cornyn 2. Ted Cruz
New Mexico	1. Martin Heinrich 2. Tom Udall	Utah	1. Mike Lee 2. Mitt Romney
New York	1. Kirsten E. Gillibrand 2. Charles E. Schumer	Vermont	1. Patrick Leahy 2. Bernard Sanders
North Carolina	1. Richard Burr 2. Thom Tillis	Virginia	1. Tim Kaine 2. Mark R. Warner
North Dakota	1. Kevin Kramer 2. John Hoeven	Washington	1. Maria Cantwell 2. Patty Murray
Ohio	1. Sherrod Brown 2. Rob Portman	West Virginia	1. Shelley Moore Capito 2. Joe Manchin III
Oklahoma	1. James M. Inhofe 2. James Lankford	Wisconsin	1. Tammy Baldwin 2. Ron Johnson
Oregon	1. Jeff Merkley 2. Ron Wyden	Wyoming	1. John Barrasso 2. Michael B. Enzi
Pennsylvania	1. Robert P. Casey, Jr. 2. Patrick J. Toomey		
Rhode Island	1. Jack Reed 2. Sheldon Whitehouse		

State Capitals (50) and Territories	10

State	Capital City
Alabama	Montgomery
Alaska	Juneau
Arizona	Phoenix
Arkansas	Little Rock
California	Sacramento
Colorado	Denver
Connecticut	Hartford
Delaware	Dover
Florida	Tallahassee
Georgia	Atlanta
Hawaii	Honolulu
Idaho	Boise
Illinois	Springfield
Indiana	Indianapolis
Iowa	Des Moines
Kansas	Topeka
Kentucky	Frankfort
Louisiana	Baton Rouge
Maine	Augusta
Maryland	Annapolis
Massachusetts	Boston
Michigan	Lansing
Minnesota	St. Paul
Mississippi	Jackson
Missouri	Jefferson City
Montana	Helena
Nebraska	Lincoln
Nevada	Carson City

State	Capital City
New Hampshire	Concord
New Jersey	Trenton
New Mexico	Santa Fe
New York	Albany
North Carolina	Raleigh
North Dakota	Bismarck
Ohio	Columbus
Oklahoma	Oklahoma City
Oregon	Salem
Pennsylvania	Harrisburg
Rhode Island	Providence
South Carolina	Columbia
South Dakota	Pierre
Tennessee	Nashville
Texas	Austin
Utah	Salt Lake City
Vermont	Montpelier
Virginia	Richmond
Washington	Olympia
West Virginia	Charleston
Wisconsin	Madison
Wyoming	Cheyenne
U.S. Territories (#)	
American Samoa	Pago Pago
Guam	Hagatna
Northern Mariana Islands	Saipan
Puerto Rico	San Juan
U.S. Virgin Islands	Charlotte Amalie

(#) Partial list

State Governors (50) and Territories	11

State	Governor
Alabama	Kay Ivey
Alaska	Michael J. Dunleavy
Arizona	Doug Ducey
Arkansas	Asa Hutchinson
California	Gavin Newsom
Colorado	Jared Polis
Connecticut	Ned Lamont
Delaware	John Carney
Florida	Ron DeSantis
Georgia	Brian P. Kemp
Hawaii	David Y. Ige
Idaho	Brad Little
Illinois	JB Pritzker
Indiana	Eric J. Holcomb
Iowa	Kim Reynolds
Kansas	Laura Kelly
Kentucky	Andy Beshear
Louisiana	John Bel Edwards
Maine	Janet Mills
Maryland	Larry Hogan
Massachusetts	Charlie Baker
Michigan	Gretchen Whitmer
Minnesota	Tim Waltz
Mississippi	Tate Reeves
Missouri	Mike Parson
Montana	Steve Bullock
Nebraska	Pete Ricketts
Nevada	Steve Sisolak

State	Governor
New Hampshire	Chris Sununu
New Jersey	Phil Murphy
New Mexico	Michelle Lujan Grisham
New York	Andrew M. Cuomo
North Carolina	Roy Cooper
North Dakota	Doug Burgum
Ohio	Mike DeWine
Oklahoma	Kevin Stitt
Oregon	Kate Brown
Pennsylvania	Tom Wolf
Rhode Island	Gina M. Raimondo
South Carolina	Henry McMaster
South Dakota	Kristi Noem
Tennessee	Bill Lee
Texas	Greg Abbott
Utah	Gary Herbert
Vermont	Phil Scott
Virginia	Ralph Northam
Washington	Jay Inslee
West Virginia	Jim Justice
Wisconsin	Tony Evers
Wyoming	Mark Gordon
U.S. Territories (#)	
American Samoa	Lolo Matalasi Moliga
Guam	Lourdes (Lou) A. Leon Guerrero
Northern Mariana Islands	Ralph DeLeon Guerrero Torres
Puerto Rico	Wanda Vasquez Garced
U.S. Virgin Islands	Albert Bryan

(#) partial list

Getting Information Online	12

The names of the 2 United States Senators from your State:

www.senate.gov

_____

The name of your state's Governor:

www. usa.gov/states-and-territories

_____

The name of your Representative and the name of the Speaker of the House of Representatives:

www.house.gov

_____

To visit the Immigration and Naturalization Services' web page, which includes information on the Naturalization (Citizenship) Test:

www.uscis.gov

_____

FREE 16-minute USCIS video
(You can see the official FREE 16-minute video which has an example of the interview by going to the following website:

https://www.uscis.gov/citizenship/learners/study-test

(In the "More Information" box on the right of the page, click on "USCIS Naturalization Interview and Test Video".

Credits

(1) "U.S. Constitution", "Thomas Jefferson" and "Abraham Lincoln" , "Constitutional Convention" (https://commons.wikimedia.org) (Public domain in the U. S.: A work prepared by an officer or employee of the U. S. Government as part of that person's official duties under terms of Title 17, Chpt. 1, Sect. 105 of US Code.)

(2) "Declaration of Independence" (https://en.wikipedia.org/wiki/United_States_Declaration_of_Independence) Public domain in the United States because it was published (or registered with the U.S. Copyright Office) before January 1, 1924.

(3) "Capitol Building " Public domain   https://upload.wikimedia.org/wikipedia/commons/thumb/b/b2/United_States_Capitol_-west_front.jpg/1280px-United_States_Capitol_-_west_front.jpg As a work of the U.S. federal government, all images created or made by the Architect of the Capitol are in the public domain in the United States.

(4) "Senate" Public domain (https://commons.wikimedia.org) As a work of the U.S. federal government, the image is in the public domain.

(5) Public domain map (https://commons.wikimedia.org) This map was obtained from an edition of the National Atlas of the United States. Like almost all works of the U.S. federal government, works from the National Atlas are in the public domain in the United States.

(6) "U.S. Supreme Court Building", "Martin Luther King", "Statue of Liberty", "American Flag", Liberty image on front cover of book, and Lady With Flag on back cover of book: Fotolia.com license

(7) "Civil War Battle" Public domain (https://commons.wikimedia.org) This work is in the public domain in the United States because it was published (or registered with the U.S. Copyright Office) before January 1, 1924.

(8) "Susan B. Anthony" . Public domain (https://commons.wikimedia.org) This media file is in the public domain in the United States. This applies to U.S. works where the copyright has expired, often because its first publication occurred prior to January 1, 1924, and if not then due to lack of notice or renewal.

(9) The Official Civics Lessons are from the USCIS official publication "Learn About the United States: Quick Civic Lessons". M-638 (rev. 02/19)

(10) Benjamin Franklin Public Domain. (https://commons.wikimedia.org) This work is in the public domain in its country of origin and other countries and areas where the copyright term is the author's life plus 100 years or less. "Faithful reproductions of two-dimensional public domain works of art are in the public domain. This photographic reproduction is therefore also considered to be in the public domain in the United States."

(11) "George Washington" (https://commons.wikimedia.org) Public domain The author died in 1828, so this work is in the public domain in its country of origin and other countries and areas where the copyright term is the author's life plus 100 years or less. This work is in the public domain in the United States because it was published (or registered with the U.S. Copyright Office) before January 1, 1924.

(12) "Dwight D. Eisenhour" Wikipedia.org Public domain. This file is a work of an employee of the Executive Office of the President of the United States, taken or made as part of that person's official duties. As a work of the U.S. federal government, it is in the public domain.

(13) Wikipedia.org Public domain This work is in the public domain in its country of origin and other countries and areas where the copyright term is the author's life plus 100 years or less. This work is in the public domain in the United States because it was published (or registered with the U.S. Copyright Office) before January 1, 1924.

POCKET-SIZED AND EASY TO USE!

The aim of this book is to be:
SIMPLE
EASY TO USE
and
POCKET-SIZED
so that you can
TAKE IT WITH YOU WHEREVER YOU GO!

This book features an **EASY ANSWER** for every one of the 100 Official USCIS civics questions.

It also includes all the reading and writing words
you need to know, and practice sentences.

It provides the web address for the

OFFICIAL and FREE 16-minute USCIS video

which has an example of the naturalization interview and suggestions on how to do it right!

Notes

Notes

Made in the USA
Columbia, SC
02 December 2020

26084788R00089